God, Pandemics, and the Holocaust

"Through his utterly gripping narration of the great pandemics of human history and the Holocaust, Cliff Cain undoes the toxic presumption that—for reasons of wrath, test, or wake-up call—God causes or permits such suffering. People of faith need Cain's infectious, indeed contagious, alternative!"

—**Catherine Keller**, George T. Cobb Professor of Constructive Theology, Drew Theological School, author of *Facing Apocalypse: Climate, Democracy and Other Last Chances*

"Using copious quotes from influential voices past and present, Cliff Cain surveys the common excuses given for why a loving and powerful God doesn't stop evil. He finds them unsatisfying. Taking the most difficult questions about evil—such as why God didn't stop COVID-19 or the Holocaust—Cain offers a solution to the problem of evil. His answer points to the unequivocal but non-controlling love of God. I highly recommend this book!"

—**Thomas Jay Oord**, author of *God Can't* and other books.

"Cliff Cain's timely book raises the existential, theological question of why God would allow pandemics to ravage the world and inflict such suffering on its people. Providing historical context, Dr. Cain considers the COVID pandemic in light of the bubonic plague, the Spanish flu, and the Holocaust. Rejecting theological appeals to God's retribution, mystery, and other such traditional responses, he challenges us to conclude that our traditional conception of God must change to one of God who loves and suffers with us rather than standing idly by staying his hand. A welcome, unique perspective for all those interested in God's relationship to our pandemic world."

—**Rich Geenen**, professor of philosophy, Westminster College of Missouri

"Most of us have had questions around God's omnipotence and human suffering. The COVID-19 epidemic and the Holocaust certainly raised the profile of those questions. Cliff Cain offers a helpful way to consider the options for responding thoughtfully and theologically to human suffering during COVID-19 and previous pandemics and during genocides. Covering biblical and historical theological responses to mass human suffering, Cain leads readers to a place where they can hold in tension God's love and the world we live in. Wherever you find yourself on this spectrum of belief, Cliff Cain's work offers a chance to sharpen your perspective and deepen your appreciation for God's love for this world."

—**Peter Henry**, minister of word and sacrament, PC (USA), pastor and head of staff, Davidson College Presbyterian Church, North Carolina

"Dr. Cliff Cain does not fear to tread into difficult waters. Here, he gathers from across the centuries, all the best (and worst) answers to the persistent question, 'How can there be God, whom we understand to be both good and omnipotent, and still evil and suffering persist?,' and offers them to his readers through the backdrop of three global pandemics—the Bubonic Plague, the Spanish Flu, and COVID-19—and the Holocaust. By the end, this modern-day theologian has guided his reader into new and freeing possibilities, and perhaps a new relationship with both God and the challenges of our human existence."

—**Caroline Dennis**, pastor, Westminster Presbyterian Church, Greenwood, South Carolina

"At a time when popular Christianity largely worships a god of bargains, with idols of certainty, comfort, and hedonism here and in the hereafter, Cliff Cain's *God, Pandemics, and the Holocaust,* gives us a stinging critique of using God for our purposes and argues forcefully for us to instead follow a God of love and compassion regardless of the consequences. It is a disturbing yet helpful book."

—**David H. Chandler**, professor of philosophy, emeritus, Franklin College of Indiana

God, Pandemics, and the Holocaust

Clifford Chalmers Cain

FOREWORD BY
Marjorie Hewitt Suchocki

WIPF & STOCK · Eugene, Oregon

GOD, PANDEMICS, AND THE HOLOCAUST

Copyright © 2025 Clifford Chalmers Cain. All rights reserved. Except for brief quotations in critical publications or reviews, no part of this book may be reproduced in any manner without prior written permission from the publisher. Write: Permissions, Wipf and Stock Publishers, 199 W. 8th Ave., Suite 3, Eugene, OR 97401.

Wipf & Stock
An Imprint of Wipf and Stock Publishers
199 W. 8th Ave., Suite 3
Eugene, OR 97401

www.wipfandstock.com

PAPERBACK ISBN: 979-8-3852-2289-6
HARDCOVER ISBN: 979-8-3852-2290-2
EBOOK ISBN: 979-8-3852-2291-9

VERSION NUMBER 02/06/25

Scripture quotations are from New Revised Standard Version Bible, copyright © 1989 National Council of the Churches of Christ in the United States of America. Used by permission. All rights reserved worldwide.

To all my formal and informal teachers through the years:
You had the kindness and persistence to teach me,
and I had the privilege and pleasure of learning from you.
I can never thank you enough.

In memory of, and in gratitude for,
the life and thought
of theologian John B. Cobb, Jr.
(1925–2024).

Contents

Foreword by Marjorie Hewitt Suchocki | ix
Preface | xiii

Chapter One: The Bubonic Plague | 1
Chapter Two: The Spanish Flu | 24
Chapter Three: COVID-19 | 38
Chapter Four: Plague, Holocaust, Tsunami, and Evolution | 55
Chapter Five: An Alternative Vision of God | 81
Chapter Six: Love as the Primary Divine Characteristic | 93

Bibliography | 119
Index | 129

Foreword

ALL THE READERS OF this volume will have survived the COVID-19 pandemic, first identified in late 2019, and rather quickly moving from China to the whole world. In the process of its interaction with the human species (on which it apparently thrives), the pathogens in this disease have been consummate "shape-shifters," experimenting with one variation after another—all of them lethal. With the help of vaccines and preventive measures such as masks, many of us have survived—but oh, the pain and heartache as we miss those who did not, and we continue to commiserate with those suffering from "long COVID" whom the disease never quite left.

Therefore, we come to this book called *God, Pandemics, and the Holocaust* with more than a sheerly academic interest, for the topic touches our lives in deep and sometimes unfathomable ways. The very reality of the pandemic becomes a religious issue in both a theological sense (how does a god/God co-exist with such massive human suffering?) and in a compassionate sense (how can each one of us comfort and absorb the pain of loss experienced by so many among us?).

Cliff Cain's book offers help in this time of pain, possibly guilt, and survival. How is a presumably loving God so viciously absent in our most heart-rending grief?

Cain begins his book holding this question at bay as he gives us a masterful history of several ghastly pandemics, each of which has caused untold suffering during its years among us. He describes one which occurred during the late years of the Roman Empire. Most Romans escaped the city, and hopefully therefore the plague—but the Christians, sometimes simply because they had nowhere else to go, stayed behind and cared for the sick in the city. As the pandemic eased and Romans returned, many were so impressed by the compassion shown by Christians that the faith began to grow. But the reality of pandemics would raise severe theological problems in the Christian world as it developed in medieval Europe.

The viciousness of plagues afflicting the European world began raising the question: Isn't God all-powerful? Then why does God permit these horrors to afflict us? In too many cases, the most compelling answer was this: God is intentionally afflicting us with the plague because we have sinned so very badly that this is the kind of punishment we deserve. And if the question of God's reputed love for us arose, it was answered with the analogy of parenthood. Parents punish their miscreant children in order to teach them "not to do that again." Punishment is therefore consistent with divine love.

Another response to the correlation of plague-as-punishment was an effort to punish ourselves, as if the severity with which we treat ourselves might mitigate God's wrath and thus hopefully end the plague. One such effort was the "flagellants" of medieval history, who went throughout the country in winter as well as summer, beating their bare backs with bunches of leather thongs, each of which had an iron "thorn" attached to its end so as to lacerate one's back unmercifully.

Yet another response for Christians was to find someone other than themselves responsible for the plague, and this "other" was invariably the Jewish people, who likewise suffered the same plague. They were "poisoning the wells," said the Christians, and therefore proceeded to punish Jews with torture and death. There was precedent indeed for the twentieth century's Holocaust, with its massive cruelty and death primarily of Jews.

No matter the immediate response to these pandemics, there was one haunting question enduring even when "punishment for our sins" was the supposed rationale. How is a God who punishes us so severely still a "loving" God? The parental analogy did not match the severity of the punishment. Did God really love?

Already in medieval theology there were questions about the "love" of a God who was necessarily considered immutable, without feeling at all, since feeling would introduce change. And while such a question could be "answered" by particularly strained notions of a love that could not admit of feeling, it wasn't until the horror of the Nazi Holocaust that sufficient pressure was put upon Christians in particular to answer the question, How is God's so-called "love" compatible with "allowing" such suffering to go on, even for years, before it finally abated, having killed many in the process of its reign? Jewish thought was not tied to Christian notions of divine impassibility, so Elie Wiesel simply denies impassibility: God is there, in the midst of the suffering, bearing it with us so that we, too, can bear it. Eventually Christian theologians, such as Jürgen Moltmann, follow suit, placing God not above the suffering, but in its midst, suffering with us.

Hence Cliff Cain's current study of God and pandemics and the Holocaust. Following his chapters masterfully detailing three pandemics and the Holocaust, he spends his final chapters on twenty-first century "answers" to what seems to be an unanswerable question. He draws upon a great variety of theologians, including Jewish and Muslim theologians, but the dominating answers come from process theologian Thomas Oord, who follows the metaphysics of Alfred North Whitehead. Oord suggests seven possible theological ways of holding divine power in tension with God's apparent inability to prevent the horrendous suffering of pandemics. The answer, suggest Oord and then Cain, is to revisit the very notion of power as a relational term—power "with" rather than power "over." "Omnipotence," as Charles Hartshorne suggests in his book *Omnipotence and Other Theological Mistakes*, is a theological mistake. We can say the same of divine impassibility.

While Cain's and Oord's work is distinctive, it represents a shift in Christian theological notions of "power" that begins in the last third of the twentieth century. Power, whether in God or in humans, is necessarily a relational term, not static. And likewise with love, it is necessarily a relational reality, not a static thing in and of itself. Impassibility, like omnipotence, is a category mistake.

It is for you, the reader, to follow these arguments to determine their success (or not) in considering the role of God and pain and suffering. For while we have survived—or seem to have survived—the COVID pandemic, history assures us that there will be others to follow.

Marjorie Hewitt Suchocki
Professor of Theology Emerita
Claremont School of Theology

Preface

THIS BOOK HAS BEEN a number of years in the making.

Although I have written other books, chiefly focusing on the intersection of theology and science or the necessary overlap between religion and ecology, I have not previously isolated and accented one of the most crucial and critical issues that has persisted throughout my professorial, writing, and pastoral career. And that is the perennial conundrum of the existence of God and the persistence of pain and suffering.

How can one reconcile the belief in an omnibenevolent (all-good), omniscient (all-knowing), and omnipotent (all-powerful) deity with the enormity and gravity of evil (pain and suffering) in the world? One of the ancient Greek philosophers, Epicurus (341–270 BCE), put it succinctly:

> Is God willing to prevent evil, but not able? Then God is not omnipotent. Is God able, but not willing? Then God is malevolent. Is God both able and willing? Then why are there evil and suffering in the world? Is God neither able nor willing? Then why call God "God"?[1]

Epicurus went on to argue that the world is *not* under the care of a loving God who providentially oversees events in the world. Epicurus believed that his mechanistic explanations of natural phenomena had no need of any appeal to divine action to account for them. The breadth and depth of suffering in the world meant that there was no God who ruled the world. However, he *did* admit that there were gods; however, these gods were "supremely blessed and happy beings." As such, they would not be concerned

---

1. Epicurus, *De Ira Dei* ("Of the Wrath of God"), 13, 20–21, in Laërtius, *Lives of the Eminent Philosophers*, book X, sections 17, 19.

about the miseries of the world nor trouble themselves with administering that world. Earthquakes, lightning, and other natural phenomena were explainable through material, atomic terms (i.e., the movement and interaction of atoms in empty space) and were not due to the will and actions of the gods. The gods have no influence on human lives.

Beyond this, Epicurus contended that the gods are not concerned about human beings and their behavior, and that happiness is its own reward, and suffering is its own punishment. The gods do not care about humans with benevolence, because otherwise evil would not exist in the world. Because suffering does exist, it must either be the case that God is not aware of everything (is not omniscient), is not all-powerful (is not omnipotent), or does not care if we suffer (is not omnibenevolent).

Or put otherwise, if God knows about our suffering (is all-knowing), cares about our suffering (is all-loving) and can do something about our suffering (is all-powerful), then there should not be any suffering! But Epicurus is challenging only *one* way of thinking about God.[2]

The matter in question has plagued every time and place. If God wills evil (pain and suffering), then God is not good, but malevolent. If God permits evil, then God's goodness and power may be maintained, but "mystery" must be invoked, since humans cannot know "why" God allows such suffering to occur (and continue, unaddressed) without divine intervention. If God does not will evil, but evil runs amok, then God is weak and unable to prevent it (does such a God deserve to be called "God?").

How was God involved in perhaps the quintessence of recent human evil, the murder of six million Jews and four million other "subhuman" undesirables (*Untermenschen*) such as Roma and Slavs during the Holocaust? Did God cause this horrible event? Was it punishment for sin? Alternately, did God tolerate it as the preservation of human freedom to choose evil as well as good? Was it an instructive lesson to be learned?

And how is God related to evolutionary theory, in which there has been tremendous waste throughout an extremely long process to arrive at our present situation, which is itself in process of development? Did God design the human eye, which sees both wonders and woes, but also the epiglottis without which we can choke to death (since the function of this

---

2. O'Keefe, "Epicurus"; Laërtius, *Lives of the Eminent Philosophers*, "Letter of Epicurus to Herodotus," book X, sections 75–76, "Letter of Epicurus to Pythocles: About the Heavenly Bodies," sections 99–116.

is to seal off the trachea when we swallow; sometimes the epiglottis does not close sufficiently during swallowing, which allows foods to enter the airways, and this can result in choking—pain and discomfort can be the consequence, as well as death! Other animals, such as insects and clams, have separate digestive and respiratory systems)?[3]

Perhaps God "set up" the world and its "laws" (biorhythms and ecocycles), but afterward withdrew and now watches "from afar" with no regulation or interference or *continua creatio* (no active presence of God for the created world's maintenance and subsistence)? Could God be an "absentee landlord" who is responsible for the world's coming-to-be, but not responsible for the "goings-on" in it?

As the third-century CE apologist Lactantius put it, to deny providence is to take away the existence of God.[4] Indeed, the Deism (God is remote, not involved in the world) of some of the philosophers and some of the scientists and some of the US presidents (such as Washington, Jefferson, Franklin, Madison, Monroe, and Tyler) relegates God to a position of transcendence as Creator, but does not reflect the biblical notion of a God who continues to "mix it up" with God's creation. The doctrine of providence is thusly sacrificed, since it seems futile to concoct a job description for God in a world that is understood to operate on its own from naturalistic causation.

And how is God connected to natural phenomena such as hurricanes, floods, wildfires, climate change, and epidemics? What does God "do" in the natural world? Are these disasters "caused" by God? "Permitted" by God? "Used" by God for another (perhaps "higher") purpose?

The unexpected onslaught of COVID has provided an opportunity and the impetus to study and reflect on "how" God might be involved in a world whose events and occurrences are largely, if not completely, analyzed and interpreted in light of science. What role, if any, can and does God play in light of human freedom, moral crises, unspeakable horrors and violence, and in light of pandemics, hurricanes, earthquakes, wildfires, and other natural catastrophes?

But, of course, COVID-19 was not the first worldwide catastrophe in terms of disease. There have been numerous outbreaks of pandemics.

---

3. Sherman and Shellman, "Intelligent Design."

4. Lactantius, "On the Anger of God," ch. 9, "Of the Providence of God, and of Opinions Opposed to It."

PREFACE

Arguably, the worst among them was the bubonic plague of the fourteenth century and the Spanish flu of the early twentieth century. As a result, *God, Pandemics, and the Holocaust* will investigate these three significant, earth-shattering, life-changing diseases. These maladies will be historically discussed, and religious responses to them will be examined. Then various ways of thinking about God and such natural evils will be considered.

In addition, reflections on the Holocaust will examine how God can be active in a world in which heinous and perverse human actions lead to tragic and unspeakable consequences. The Holocaust perhaps represents the epitome of such evil, resulting in the near extinction of European Jewry and other persons viewed to be of no value and therefore expendable. Did God cause such events? Permit them? Watch them detachedly from afar? Genuinely suffer with the victims in their terror and pain, helpless to do anything to assist?

Efforts to answer these questions will be primarily directed toward a lay audience, as well as to fellow scholars. It is likely that all persons, whether people on the street, Christians in the pews, or theologians and pastors in their studies, have been impacted by these issues and attempted to address them.

In this endeavor, a number of people, both quite knowingly and also undoubtedly unknowingly, have contributed their insights and reactions. It is perilous to make a list of them because someone could unintentionally be left out. Be that as it may, grateful thanks are extended to Marjorie Suchocki, Thomas Jay Oord, Catherine Keller, David Chandler, Caroline and Phillip Dennis, Peter Henry, Rich Geenen, Tom Pitts, John and Andrea Langton, John Uldrick, David Collins, Bob and Lorena Cowles, Wayne Zade, Ashley and Mary Woodiwiss, Don and Meg Shuler, Kyle and Christie Hite, Johan Christian Beker, Ted and Joanne Hardgrove, Brad and Gloria Christie, Bob and Annie Bailey, David and Amy Jennings, Rob and Joan Erickson, Frank Minton, Dave Henry, J. Edward Barrett, Carolyn Perry Hunt, William L. McClelland, Daniel Migliore, Keith and Shelley Hardeman, Jay B. McDaniel, Lloyd and Jan Hunter, George S. Hendry, John B. Cobb, Jr., Edward Farley, Hendrikus Berkhof, Bernhard W. Anderson, Bishop John A. T. Robinson, George Stroup, Melissa Hatfield, Osamu Nagami, and last but not least, Rachel, Zachary, and Madison Cain, and

PREFACE

certainly Nancy Poffenbaugh. Special thanks are also given to Managing Editor Matthew Wimer, Copyeditor Elisabeth Rickard, Typesetter Calvin Jaffarian, and Cover Designer Savanah Landerholm. These persons would not necessarily agree with all of the positions, claims, and contentions I offer. But because of their suggestions, criticisms, encouragement, and support, these scholars, pastors, friends, relatives, and publisher representatives have made this book better.

Clifford Chalmers Cain
Greenwood, South Carolina
Ash Wednesday, 2025

Chapter One

The Bubonic Plague

ARGUABLY THE DEADLIEST PANDEMIC in history, and "one of the greatest natural disasters ever to afflict humanity,"[1] the medieval bubonic plague emerged in the fourteenth century CE:

> Between 1346 and 1353, this disease . . . swept across Europe from the east in a clockwise motion, tightening around the medieval world like a noose. When it was over, at least half of the population was dead, 25–50 million.[2]

As but one example, in Avignon, France, 400 persons died daily over a period of three months. This totaled 36,000 dead in 90 days out of a population of 50,000.[3] In retrospect called the "Black Death," but at the time termed the "Great Mortality" or the "Great Pestilence,"[4] the bubonic plague terrorized the European populace, most of whom were Christians.[5]

Of course, this was not the first outbreak of the Great Pestilence. Perhaps most notably, there was a pandemic in the reign of Emperor Justinian, who ruled in the Late Roman (or Byzantine) Empire for roughly four decades. That outbreak of the plague occurred in 541 CE and recurred

---

1. Doubleday, *After the Plague*, 1.
2. Dorsey Armstrong, *Black Death*, 1; Aberth, *From the Brink*.
3. Kreis, "Satan Triumphant."
4. Dorsey Armstrong, *Black Death*, 4.
5. Dorsey Armstrong, *Black Death*, 5.

in episodic waves until 750 CE, a period of over two centuries. Justinian himself contracted the plague, but it did not cause his death.[6] The death toll was higher than that of COVID-19, with a 60–80 percent mortality rate.[7] For example, 10,000 people were dying a day in the capital city of Constantinople.[8]

The second outbreak was the one referenced in the fourteenth century, and then there was a third pandemic in the nineteenth century (beginning in 1894 in Asia). As scientists have pointed out, the bubonic plague is a disease that goes back even further, as the bacterium *Yersinia pestis*, the pathogen that causes it, has been detected in the remains of human beings from 6,500 years ago.[9]

The first plague mentioned, the Justinian Plague, was interpreted by religious leaders of the time as "divine punishment for man's many sins."[10] There would be a very similar theological interpretation regarding the second outbreak beginning in 1346. Starting in Asia, the bubonic plague made its way to Europe partially through the siege of the city of Caffa (now Feodosia) in the Ukraine. The Mongols lifted the siege twice, the second time because their forces were devastated by an epidemic of the plague:

> Oh God! See how the heathen Tartar [Mongol] races, pouring together from all sides, suddenly infested the city of Caffa and besieged the trapped Christians there for almost three years.... But behold, the whole army was affected by a disease which overran the Tartars and killed thousands upon thousands every day.... It was as though arrows were raining down from heavens to strike and crush the Tartars' arrogance. All medical advice and attention was useless; the Tartars died as soon as the signs of the disease appeared on their bodies—swellings in the armpit or groin... followed by a putrid fever.[11]

But before withdrawal, the Mongol leader, Janibeg, had plague-stricken corpses catapulted over the city walls in what has been called "the most

---

6. Sessa, "Justinianic Plague."
7. Sessa, "Justinianic Plague."
8. Dorsey Armstrong, *Black Death*, 16.
9. Sessa, "Justinianic Plague."
10. John of Ephesus, Christian bishop, in Sessa, "Justinianic Plague"; see also Meier, "'Justinianic Plague,'" 267–92.
11. De' Mussi, *Historia de Morbo*, 14.

spectacular incident of biological warfare ever."[12] These cadavers spread the bubonic plague to Italians within the city of Caffa, and from there the fleeing inhabitants took it to Europe (Mediterranean ports). Other routes to Europe were also used, but "sailors and merchants primarily from the Italian peninsula brought it into the European world."[13]

Public reactions to the plague (families fleeing stricken members, mass graves, priests reticent to attend to victims, etc.), including initial theological responses, were noted by a person from Genoa, Italy, Gabriele de' Mussi (ca. 1280–ca. 1356), whose writing is presumed to have been in late 1348 or early 1349. His description "begins with an apocalyptic speech by God, lamenting the depravity to which humanity has fallen and describing the retribution intended."[14] Dr. Mark Wheelis, a microbiologist whose latest research has focused on biological weapons, concludes that "the plague appears to have been spread in a stepwise fashion, on many ships rather than on a few, taking a year [not just a few weeks or a few months by fleeing Italians from Caffa] to reach Europe from the Crimea," and therefore de' Mussi's account is not accurate and satisfactory. But the theological notation he makes is pertinent here:

> Medieval society lacked a coherent theory of disease causation: Three notions coexisted in a somewhat contradictory mixture, [among them and first] disease was a divine punishment for individual or collective transgression.[15]

The plague, then, was foremost (though not solely) interpreted as an act of God. For almost everyone, the plague signified the wrath of God. It was an action warranted by human sin, for which judgment had been made, and punishment had now been meted out.

> Collective trauma unleashed a conviction that God was punishing humanity for its sins . . . God's wrath was clearly so great that God had decided not to spare even the innocents: Children had perished in their millions, along with their parents. A black cloud of guilt had descended on 14th century Europe.[16]

---

12. Wheelis, "Biological Warfare," 971.
13. Dorsey Armstrong, *Black Death*, 27.
14. Wheelis, "Biological Warfare," 971.
15. De' Mussi, *Historia de Morbo*, 14–26.
16. Kreis, "Satan Triumphant"; see also Doubleday, *After the Plague*, 202.

Art historian Anna Louise DesOrmeaux adds that since God had caused the plague to punish people for their sins, there was nothing that people could do but "turn humbly to God, who never denies His aid."[17] But even at that, God seemed to deny God's aid, for the plague continued to spread and kill.

Of course, the bubonic plague did not emerge in a vacuum. There was in the previous century in 1257, "the largest volcanic eruption in the last 7,000 years." This catastrophic event in Indonesia on the island of Lombok at the Samalas volcano registered a "probable 7" on the Volcanic Explosivity Index and caused a "volcanic winter" and cooling of the atmosphere for several years.[18] This resulted in crop failures in Europe and elsewhere and subsequently famine. The Great Famine of 1315–17 affected most of Europe and ended a period of growth and prosperity that had characterized the eleventh to the thirteenth centuries.[19]

Further pressing millions of Europeans into starvation, the Great Cattle Plague, which reached central Europe in 1316, quickly became a global event, and two-thirds of the cattle were killed. Future waves of the disease struck in the 1320s and 1330s.[20]

Flooding was also a frequent phenomenon of the Middle Ages, and there were major flooding events in the thirteenth and fourteenth centuries. In fact,

> it rained almost constantly throughout the summer and autumn of 1314 and then through most of 1315 and 1316. Crops rotted in the ground, harvests failed, and livestock drowned or starved.[21]

Finally, earthquakes "shook the European continent in the years preceding and during the Black Death"[22] and were connected to the outbreaks of the bubonic plague: In January of 1348, there was seismic activity in Austria, southern Germany, and northern Italy. An earthquake also struck Italy again in 1349 during the plague. The Greek physician, philosopher, and writer Galen of Pergamum (129–ca. 216 CE) believed that the fissures

---

17. DesOrmeaux, "Black Death and Its Effect," 1641.
18. Malawani et al., "1257 CE Cataclysmic Eruption," 6–7.
19. Lucas, "Great European Famine," 343–77.
20. Doubleday, *After the Plague*, 88–89.
21. Ben Johnson, "Great Flood and Great Famine."
22. Doubleday, *After the Plague*, 82.

created by earthquakes released toxic gases into the atmosphere, creating *miasmas* (bad air), and these could lead to diseases.[23]

Since "natural disasters and epidemic disease were quite often perceived as divine punishment for sins,"[24] clergy led barefoot processions to demonstrate humility before a God whose righteousness had been offended by human transgressions, said frequent prayers and presided over additional Masses, and instructed the people to appeal to saints to protect them; people also wore amulets believed to ward off disease and protect them from disaster.[25]

As indicated, people were encouraged by church authorities to seek the protection of the saints.

> Saints were intercessors, but they were also those who enlightened the imagination of those suffering the plague, enabling them to see Christian hope in occasions of infinite sorrow.[26]

Some examples from the enormous number of "plague saints" are St. Michael, St. George, St. Sebastian, the Virgin Mary, St. Catherine, St. Roch, and St. Guinefort.

Among them, St. Michael, the defender of Jews in the Hebrew Bible/Christian Old Testament, is featured prominently in the book of Revelation in the Christian New Testament: He defeats Satan/the devil (depicted as a dragon). Here the very quintessence of evil and sin—Satan—is conquered by St. Michael; he is flung from heaven to earth and thereby dispatched. So, no matter what manner of death and suffering occurred in a city or town, one could be reassured that one's eternal salvation was assured.

Timothy O'Malley examines one painting of St. Michael—Gerard Davis's 1510 creation, *Michaelsaltar*—and notes the dark clouds (a frequent symbolic depiction of the plague) above St. Michael, who in the center defeats Satan as a dragon. In addition, in the celebration of the Eucharist in the present moment, St. Michael defeats Satan anew. To a people desperate for hope, this encouragement was crucial. St. Michael therefore became a coveted plague saint.[27]

---

23. Nutton, "Galen."
24. Doubleday, *After the Plague*, 80.
25. Doubleday, *After the Plague*, 80.
26. O'Malley, "Saints of the Black Death."
27. O'Malley, "Saints of the Black Death."

St. George (born third century CE in Cappadocia, modern-day Turkey), who also killed a dragon (as the result of a bargain he made with non-Christians: "I will kill the dragon if you will convert to becoming Christian"), was a saint whom people believed was one of the "Fourteen Holy Helpers" who could render assistance during epidemic diseases. So, "St. George's protection was invoked against . . . the Plague and leprosy."[28]

St. Sebastian, patron saint of plague victims, did not begin with this status:[29] A third-century CE Roman military officer (who rose to the rank of captain of the guard and imperial officer and finally Praetorium Guard to protect the emperor, Diocletian, 245–316; ruled 284–305) and eventual martyr, Sebastian was shot full of arrows for clinging to his faith and for converting others to Christianity (though he did not die from this event) and later clubbed to death for criticizing Emperor Diocletian's "sins," i.e., his cruelty to Christians. Arrows, like dark clouds mentioned above, were a symbol of the plague: The arrows were "an image of divine wrath, inflicted upon humankind."[30] St. Sebastian's martyrdom was reflective of Christ's so many years before: He was bound (like Christ), tied to a pole (like Christ on the cross), led like a lamb (akin to Christ as "the Lamb of God, who takes away the sins of the world") to the slaughter, and within the legend, is rescued from death in a "resurrection" (St. Irene, according to the story, miraculously removed the arrows and healed his wounds). So, death was "configured to the sacrifice of Christ," and death from the plague could become interpreted as a "sacrificial offering."[31]

St. Sebastian was believed to play a role in the lifting of a plague in 680 CE in the city of Pavia, Italy, when a man was told that the plague would not subside until an altar to St. Sebastian was built in Rome at the Basilica of St. Peter in Vincoli. The plague lifted at the very moment that the altar was constructed. To "invoke once again the intercession of St. Sebastian, the one who confirmed himself perfectly to Christ," was to grab hold of hope in a seemingly hopeless situation. The cult of St. Sebastian was centered in Rome (he became the third patron saint of the city), and his body and the arrows became "a consolation for those who suffered or lost those in the plague."[32]

28. O'Malley, "Saints of the Black Death."
29. Barker, "Making of a Plague Saint," 90–127.
30. O'Malley, "Saints of the Black Death."
31. O'Malley, "Saints of the Black Death."
32. O'Malley, "Saints of the Black Death."

English historian Rosemary Horrox asserts that the Virgin Mary, who "was regularly invoked against the plague and its terrors, and the image of her as the Mother of Mercy, shielding mankind with her cloak," was extremely powerful to the faithful.[33] Mary was seen as a "benefactor" to relieve persons from the wrath of God as perceived in the plague. She would be an intercessor, but equally she could identify with the pain and suffering of those afflicted by the plague. The mother of Jesus, who is depicted in some paintings of the time as fainting when Jesus is taken down from the cross, identifies with mothers and fathers who have lost their children as well.

> Mary was therefore the Mother of Mercy, the one who took upon herself all of human suffering alongside her Son. Because she attuned herself to the tender compassion of her Son as beloved Mother, she could intervene for all those who suffer.[34]

St. Catherine of Siena (1347–90), though she lost three siblings and other relatives in a plague that struck Siena, Italy, did not flee the city as most did, but stayed behind to nurse victims.[35] Catherine did not interpret the plague as the product of God's wrath; instead, she saw it, whatever its cause, as an opportunity to demonstrate the sacrificial love of Christ to those who were suffering.[36]

St. Roch was born (ca. 1350) to French parents. When the plague struck Venice with a vengeance, a cult sprang up beginning in the fifteenth century around the figure of St. Roch, who offered comfort to those suffering the immense amount of death around them.[37] Since commentators contemporary to the plague assumed it had "supernatural origins, acting as a punishment from God against a sinful population,"[38] they believed that "those suffering from the plague, fleeing to the protection of Roch, will escape that most violent contagion."[39] Roch, on a journey to Rome, had stopped at a town en route that was beset by the plague, and placing his own life and welfare at risk (and to the astonishment of the medical

---

33. Horrox, *Black Death*, 97.
34. O'Malley, "Saints of the Black Death."
35. Catherine of Siena, *Letters*, 48–210.
36. Catherine of Siena, *Letters*, 48–210.
37. Sweeney, "Salvation in a Time of Plague."
38. Marshall, *Waiting on the Will*.
39. Vaslef, *Role of St. Roch*.

personnel), rushed into the hospital and began caring for the sick and suffering. He himself would contract the plague, but he survived, so the story goes, by withdrawing to the forest (and thereby practicing a form of social distancing), where he was ministered to by a spring of water that appeared and by a dog that brought him daily food (bread) and licked his sores. Roch continued to help persons through "miraculous healings" by traveling to homes of poor people and to hospitals where the plague-stricken were located. This sacrificial service was imitated by others who were inspired by Roch's example.

Desperate situations require desperate measures, and the plague constituted a desperate situation: So, as an extreme measure by today's sensibilities, a dog was venerated as a saint and appeals to it were common enough to label this phenomenon as a "cult." St. Guinefort was a "legendary thirteenth century French greyhound that received local veneration as a folk saint."[40] According to the legend, a knight living near Lyon, France, wrongly suspected his dog, Guinefort the greyhound, of having killed his infant son since the child was missing and the dog's jaws were bloody. In anger, the knight slew the dog only to discover that the dog had killed a poisonous snake (hence the blood on the dog's mouth) that had threatened the son, and the son was safe under his overturned cradle. Clearly, Guinefort was a hero and innocent, but he had been martyred. So, the knight's family buried the dog in a well, covered it with stones, and planted trees around it. Locals then venerated the dog as a saint, and mothers would visit the shrine of trees especially with sick children needing to be cured. Thirteenth-century Dominican friar Stephen of Bourbon (d. 1262) first described the story in 1250 and observed:

> The local peasants hearing of the dog's noble deed and innocent death, began to visit the place and honor the dog as a martyr in quest of help for their sicknesses and other needs.[41]

Pilgrimages were also a mainstream response to the plague. It's estimated that in the fourteenth-century year of the plague, 500,000 pilgrims visited Santiago de Compostela alone. Nevertheless, it was Jerusalem that was regarded as the highest pilgrimage site, with Rome in second place. Although Jubilee Years were to be proclaimed only one time per century (with the previous one declared for 1300 by Pope Boniface VIII), Pope Clement VI

---

40. Schmitt, *Holy Greyhound*.
41. Stephen of Bourbon, *De Supersticione*.

called a Jubilee for 1350 (during the plague), and for those who would journey on pilgrimage to Rome and visit St. Peter's and St. Paul's Basilicas once a day for fifteen days, they would receive full forgiveness for all their sins and thereby "get a ticket on the express train out of purgatory."[42]

Pilgrims also went to smaller shrines, like the tomb of Thomas Becket. This was located at Canterbury in the county of Kent, England, and was the destination of the band of pilgrims in Geoffrey Chaucer's *Canterbury Tales*. Pilgrims also went to Norfolk, England, to witness the Virgin Mary's breast milk.

Regardless of spiritual destination, pilgrims wore blue robes and wide-brimmed hats, plus a bottle for water and a pouch for food and money, and maybe a religious book. Their robes doubled as sleeping bags at night. It has been reported that pilgrims would wear metal badges—some of them ridiculously erotic—to ward off the plague and also as proof that they had visited the various spiritual destinations. But the badges were more than just pewter; they were also believed to contain power to ward off disease and to heal disease: Touching the badge to a tomb or close to a holy relic charged that keepsake with spiritual power.[43]

The flagellant movement was yet another religious response to the plague: The flagellant movement emerged in 1348 CE in Austria (some scholars say in Hungary as well) and spread in the next year to Germany and Flanders. Flagellants roamed from town to city to countryside whipping themselves for their sins and for the sins of humanity. Although the movement would be banned by Pope Clement VI (1291–1352) as ineffectual, disruptive, and heretical, it became quite popular as the church's power and influence fell into disrepute (nothing the church prescribed or suggested seemed to "work") and as people became increasingly desperate for an or any "answer" for how to make the plague go away.[44]

Psychiatrist Norman Doidge points out in his article "Plague as Punishment" that historian Norman Cohn, in his comprehensive history of the flagellant movement and of millenarianism (*The Pursuit of the Millennium*), argues that the first phase of the flagellant movement began in 1260 in Italy after an outbreak of the plague in 1259. The second emergence of the flagellant movement occurred in 1348. We know some of what the flagellants were thinking, says Cohn, because their creed was written out in "The

---

42. Dorsey Armstrong, *Black Death*, 127.
43. Campbell, "Medieval Pilgrims Apparently."
44. Doubleday, *After the Plague*, 202–3.

Heavenly Letter," which stated that God himself had inscribed a marble tablet with a message for humanity, explaining why the plague had come:

> God was angry at humanity for its many sins and blasphemies, and the plague and famine were to be humankind's punishment. He had decided to kill every last living thing on Earth. But, hearing His threat, the Virgin Mary and the angels fell at His feet and implored Him to give humanity one last chance to mend their ways. God was moved. So, the angel appeared to bid mankind to embark on the flagellation processions and purify themselves.[45]

This urgency meant that the self-chastising purification had to be very extreme.

Professor Steven Kreis of the American Public University provides an excellent, full summary of the extreme and ritualistic activities of the flagellant movement:

> Processions of men, initially well-organized, walked two by two, chanting their *Pater Nosters* and *Ave Marias* . . . and [summoned] the townspeople to the marketplace. At the head of the procession were the Master and his two lieutenants who carried banners of purple velvet and cloths of gold. The marchers were silent, their heads and faces hidden, and their eyes were fixed on the ground before them . . . church bells would ring and announce their arrival. The marchers, once they had arrived, would strip to the waist and form a large circle. The flagellants marched around the perimeter of the circle and at the order of the Master, would throw themselves to the ground. The Master walked among them, beating those who had committed crimes or who had violated the discipline of the Brotherhood. Following this ceremony, the collective flagellation took place. Each brother carried a heavy leather thong, tipped with metal studs. With this they began to beat themselves and others. Three Brethren acted as cheerleaders while the Master prayed for God's mercy on all sinners . . . . The public ceremony was repeated twice a day and once at night for a period of thirty-three and a half days! [each day referred to a year of Jesus's earthly life] . . . The flagellant movement was well-regulated and sternly disciplined. New entrants (mostly laymen and unbeneficed clergy) had to make a confession of all sins since the age of seven and then flagellate themselves for thirty-three and a half days. Each member also vowed never to bathe, shave, sleep in a bed, change their clothing or converse in any way with

---

45. Quoted in Doidge, "Plague as Punishment."

members of the opposite sex. If that wasn't enough, they also had to pay a small fee! . . . By 1349, the flagellant movement came into conflict with the Church at Rome. This clash was perhaps inevitable. After all, the Masters were claiming that they could purge sinners of their sins, something the Church claimed it could do alone . . . . Numerous princes in France and in Germany began to prohibit the entrance of the Brotherhood into their provinces. Masters were burned alive, and the flagellants were denounced by the clergy. By 1350, the flagellant movement vanished almost as quickly as it had appeared.[46]

Since medical authorities acknowledged that they were powerless to counter the plague if/since it came as a result of God's will, and because the church's admonitions and prescriptions were anemic and did not seem to cause the plague to abate, "what gave the [flagellant] movement a popular flavor was that not only individual Flagellants were thereby immune to the disease, but [also] towns that welcomed them could share in their penitential benefits."[47] Since the flagellants identified with Jesus's suffering, one townsperson exclaimed, "So much evil was changed to good when the penitents arrived."[48]

The flagellant movement also looked forward to the approaching end time, when "Christ would come, the Black Death would end, and a new age would dawn."[49] The flagellants were not the only ones adopting such an apocalyptic stance: Others concluded that all these maladies pointed to the end time. Some proclaimed that, as a prelude to the apocalypse, God was punishing people in the same way that God had punished Sodom and Gomorrah (Gen 19:24–25; cf. Deut 29:21–23; Matt 10:14–15, 11:20–24; Luke 17:28–30; Rom 9:29; 2 Pet 2:4–10; Jude 1:7; Rev 11:7–8). God utilized the bubonic plague in the fourteenth century just the way God had used other natural means such as "sulfur and fire" regarding the evil twin cities.

Thus, the "signs of the times" indicated that the thousand-year reign of Christ (the "millennium") was coming. But first, the Antichrist would appear and persecute Christians. The plague provided "evidence" for this. Eventually, the last judgment would occur, and those enemies of Christ who were not among those converted during the millennium would now be served their just desserts. In the present moment, the persecution of

46. Kreis, "Satan Triumphant."
47. Aberth, *From the Brink*, 155.
48. Horrox, *Black Death*, 150; cf. Aberth, *From the Brink*, 134, 157.
49. Gottfried, *Black Death*, 72.

Christians by the onslaught of the plague was "proof" that the reign of Christ in the millennium would be coming, and the first installment of this would arrive soon![50] This expectation also gave reassurance that everything that was happening was a part of God's divine plan (Rev 20:1–15). Historian Norman Cohn wrote comprehensively on outbreaks among Christians of such a mystical millenarianism—a vision that "after Christ's Second Coming, he would establish a messianic kingdom on earth and would reign over it for a thousand years before the Last Judgment."[51]

Even the "science" of the time seemed to support this: The king of France, Philip VI (1293–1350), called upon the forty-six masters of medicine of the impressive faculty of the University of Paris to determine what was going on. Their scientific work—*Compendium de epidemia per collegium facultatis medicorum Parisius*—was published in 1348. The *Compendium* specified that the plague was caused by numerous factors, among them earthquakes, floods, unseasonable weather, *miasma* (bad air), and a triple conjunction of the planets. It was believed that God could act, and has now acted, through natural phenomena, including the movement of stars and planets. So, when Jupiter, Mars, and Saturn aligned in the fortieth degree of Aquarius on March 20, 1345, it was concluded that this drew up the vapors from the earth—corrupt, evil vapors which destroy life force when humans breathe them in. Additionally, it was concluded that the sky had been reddened because of these vapors, and it was noted that there had been earthquakes, lightning, and thunder. Further, dead fish and animals had been discovered along the coast. So here, apocalypticism was perceived to merge with a rational cause for the occurrence of the plague. The plague was interpreted as a key "player" in the divine unfolding of history. When Pope Clement VI, in Avignon, France (where the papacy resided from 1309–77), consulted his large medical and scientific staff there, he was also told that the outbreak of the plague was caused in part by a "planetary conjunction."[52]

"Science" also proposed some "remedies": The "Vicary Method" involved plucking the back and rear end of a chicken and applying it to the swollen nodes to draw out the disease from the patient. Or one could kill a snake, chop it up, and rub the pieces over the swollen buboes (the snake being symbolic for Satan, and evil would draw out evil). Pigeons could be used

50. Ehrman, "First Lecture."
51. Quoted in Doidge, "Plague as Punishment."
52. Dorsey Armstrong, *Black Death*, 58.

the same way as snakes. Sitting close to a fire or to a sewer would pull away the bad air that caused one's sickness. Eating or drinking crushed emeralds (for poorer folks, arsenic or mercury) would alleviate the plague. Gold could also be used in the same way. "Four Thieves Vinegar" (consisting of cider, vinegar, or wine mixed with spices such as sage, clover, rosemary, and wormwood) could be consumed. "Theriac" (eighty ingredients, including opium) could be taken. Bloodletting (bleeding the blood vessel closest to the location of the swelling) could be administered. Bathing in or drinking urine could be tried. Fumigating homes with incense or carrying flowers to ward off stench and also fumigating one's lungs could be efficacious.[53]

In some cases and in some circles, the figure of the devil was invoked: As previously noted, especially in the case of St. Michael, the devil was depicted as a dragon or snake that had perpetrated the plague. Although a "fallen angel," the devil's power was formidable, and thus, God and the devil were locked in a cosmic battle. But "asymmetrical dualism" was the prevalent schematic, with God having the ultimate and final "upper hand." So, though the devil was the source of the plague, the devil was an evil agent of God, administering punishment and also tempting the afflicted and unafflicted to line up with Satan's cosmic force versus God.

Here, God is not seen as directly responsible for the plague but ultimately is in control and therefore is finally culpable. The question of why God would allow *so much* suffering and death was answered by descriptions of just how evil and sinful human beings had become. Since God permitted such extensive loss of life through the power of the devil to inflict plague, humans must have somehow deserved it. And in the long run, such tragedy would fit somehow and mysteriously into God's overarching plan: The plague was a product of God's will.

Another religious reaction turned to scapegoating. "The medieval act of 'scapegoating' was frequently used to remedy the chaos that ensued in the aftermath of disaster."[54] It was widely believed that the Jews were responsible for the plague: "A kind of Jewish evil was the source of the disturbance in the natural order and the contamination of the Christian world."[55] So, if the Jews would vanish, perhaps the plague would vanish, too.[56] Since it was commonly assumed that the Jews not only killed Christ (the charge of

53. Mark, "Medieval Cures for the Black Death."
54. Nirenberg, "Communities of Violence," 111.
55. Foa, *Jews of Europe*, 17.
56. Ziegler, *Black Death*, 74.

deicide) so long ago in the first century, but also stubbornly and arrogantly refuse to acknowledge him as the Messiah (Christ) and accept his message of salvation today in the fourteenth century, perhaps by Christians "paying back" the Jews, God would be appeased because Christians would be doing God's bidding and thereby would gain God's favor. Thus, killing Jews was an action viewed as "pleasing to God." George Kohn writes:

> In places, the plague was blamed on cripples, nobles, [lepers,] and Jews, who were accused of poisoning public wells and were either driven away or killed by fire or torture.[57]

"Lepers" were involved, because it was believed that in some cases it was they who poisoned those wells, but only after being bribed by Jews to do so.[58] And after a Jewish doctor confessed, under torture, that a boy had brought poisonous powder to him from Spain in order to infect wells, that "forced admission" spread as fast as the plague and elevated anti-Jewish sentiment even higher.[59]

Co-existing with the suffering and deaths of the plague—believed to be perpetrated by Jews—was the accomplice notion that the reason the Jews brought about the plague was to fulfill an ambition to rid the world of Christians. So, in order to avert this plot, Christians should plan to eradicate the Jews "before this conspiracy could be made a [fuller] reality."[60]

> [The townspeople], petitioning for the expulsion of the Jews, affirmed that their danger to the community extended far beyond an occasional child murder [the charge of *blood libel*, in which it was believed that Jews kidnapped Christian children, killed them, and then used their blood ritually in the preparation of *matzah* bread, especially at the time of the Passover meal], for they dry the blood they thus secure, grind it to a powder, and scatter it in the fields early in the morning when there is a heavy dew on the ground; then in three or four weeks a plague descends on men and cattle, within a radius of half a mile, so that Christians suffer severely while the sly Jews remain safely indoors.[61]

---

57. Kohn, *Encyclopedia of Plague and Pestilence*, entry 32.
58. Ziegler, *Black Death*, 72; cf. Zentner, "Black Death and Its Impact," 46.
59. Gottfried, *Black Death*, 52; Zentner, "Black Death and Its Impact," 59.
60. Zentner, "Black Death and Its Impact," 44.
61. Trachtenberg, *Devil and the Jews*, 44, quoted in Mark, "Religious Responses to the Black Death."

The persecution of Jews began in southeastern France. In Savoy, in September, 1348, the first trial was held against Jews:

> Their property was confiscated while they remained in jail. Confessions were obtained by torture, and eleven Jews were burned at the stake. At Basel in Switzerland (January 9, 1349), several hundred Jews were burned alive in a house specially constructed for this purpose. A decree was passed that ordered that no Jew could settle in Basel for two hundred years. In February, 1349, the Jews of Strasburg, numbering two thousand, were taken to the burial ground and burned at the stake *en masse*. And, in early 1349, at Mainz in Germany, Jews took the initiative and killed two hundred Christians. The Christian revenge was horrible—12,000 Jews were slaughtered.[62]

"Between 1347 and 1351, there were recorded more than 350 massacres [of Jews]."[63] It has been pointed out that secular rulers were involved as well, for example Emperor Charles IV, who "protected any bishops or knights who took part in [Jewish] executions,"[64] and Frederic of Thuringia (a state in central Germany), who declared that he had "burnt his Jews for the honor of God."[65]

Of course, the scapegoating of Jews was not performed in a vacuum, because the church had already issued thirteenth- and fourteenth-century laws that isolated them. Jews had been forced to wear a yellow badge in the shape of a coin by the dictates of the Fourth Lateran Council (1215), certain occupations were off limits (e.g., baking, carpentry, shoemaking, mining, weaving, etc.), intermarriage was forbidden, new synagogues could not be built, and Jews could not employ Christian servants.

In some locations, entire Jewish populations were murdered; in others, the numbers were severely reduced. The Jewish population of Spain and Portugal was drastically decreased to a quarter of its original size.[66] Some cities, such as Zurich, burned the Jews and then banned Jews permanently.[67] As the cause of the terrible plague and the source of an evil

---

62. Nohl, *Black Death*, 182.
63. Mark, "Medieval Cures for the Black Death."
64. Cohn Jr., "Black Death and the Burning," 15, quoted in Zentner, "Black Death and Its Impact," 55.
65. Ziegler, *Black Death*, 78, quoted in Zentner, "Black Death and Its Impact," 55.
66. Gottfried, *Black Death*, 53; cf. Zentner, "Black Death and Its Impact," 57.
67. Zentner, "Black Death and Its Impact," 54,

conspiracy plot to annihilate all Christians, Jews "deserved to be swallowed up in the flames." In fact, one of the songs that flagellants sang in their processions and rituals contained the following lyrics:

> Plague ruled the common people and overthrew many,
> The earth quaked.
> The people of the Jews is burnt,
> A strange multitude of half-naked men beat themselves.[68]

Interestingly, and ironically, during the years of bubonic plague, literature flourished. The Italian poet Francesco Petrarca (anglicized as "Petrarch"; lived 1304–74), suffered personal loss from the plague: His brother was likely the only survivor, along with his dog, at the monastery of Monrieux. And Laura, the unattainable love of his life, upon whom he first gazed on Good Friday, April 6, 1327, died from the plague twenty-one years to the day (and hour) in 1348. His son also succumbed to the plague in 1361 during a second outbreak, but Petrarch remained resilient and embraced stoicism in response to his grief. "He accepted the plague with resignation because it was deserved."[69] As the plague ranged in Parma, he wrote,

> In what annals has it ever been read the houses were left vacant, cities deserted, the country neglected, the fields too small for the dead and a fearful and universal solitude over the whole earth? . . . Oh happy people of the future, who have not known these miseries and perchance will class our testimony with fables. We have, indeed deserved these [punishments] and even greater; but our forefathers also have deserved them, and may our posterity not also merit the same."[70]

Aware that "wherever I turn my frightening eyes, their gaze is troubled by continual funerals,"[71] Petrarch led a life of piety, believing that utterly sinful persons needed to repent of their sins by "acknowledging and echoing Christ's self-sacrifice for humanity."[72] Though some questioned God's exis-

---

68. Cohn Jr., "Black Death and the Burning," 17. It is interesting to note that the Spanish flu pandemic would also give rise to a conspiracy theory that the Germans caused it, and the COVID-19 pandemic would also result in an allegation that the Chinese maliciously caused it.
69. Doidge, "Plague as Punishment."
70. Doidge, "Plague as Punishment."
71. Doubleday, *After the Plague*, 193.
72. Doubleday, *After the Plague*, 193.

tence in the aftermath of the plague, and some also skipped worship practices as an expression of skepticism or indifference, many people become more intense in their Christian faith: Petrarch was one of them.[73]

Italian poet Giovanni Boccaccio (1313–75) was born in Florence and was in his mid-thirties when the plague struck. Boccaccio suffered personally at that time, for he lost his father, his second stepmother, a number of his friends, and also possibly his uncle.[74] He also enjoyed a friendship with Petrarch, but Boccaccio's writing is more humorous and bawdier than his friend's, according to historian Simon Doubleday.[75]

In Boccaccio's masterpiece, the *Decameron*, seven women and three men leave Florence for their country villa for ten days' time.[76] Each of them takes a turn each night, save weekends, telling stories in the garden, so there are one hundred in all, and hence the title of the book. In his introduction to the *Decameron*, Boccaccio shares how Florentines during the plague had become terrified and panicked at the prospect of rendering aid to their neighbors and even parents to their children. People refused, and people fled.

In one of the stories, two lovers pledge themselves to each other, only to have dreams that involve ominous "black shapes." Though the male lover, Gabriotto, laughs this off, he suddenly dies and is buried by his female lover, Andriola. Here the lovers' dreams represent the fear of the suddenness of death, persistently present in medieval times, but even more so in the time of the plague.

In the *Decameron*, Boccaccio remarks in the opening lines that

> I say, then, that the years of the fruitful Incarnation of the Son of God had attained to the number of one thousand three hundred and forty-eight, when into the notable city of Florence, fair over every other of Italy, there came death-dealing pestilence, which, through the operation of the heavenly bodies or of our own iniquitous doings, being sent down upon mankind for our correction by the just wrath of God, had some years before appeared in the parts of the East and after having bereft these latter of an innumerable number of inhabitants, extending without cease from one place to another, had now unhappily spread towards the West.[77]

73. Doubleday, *After the Plague*, 191–92.
74. Doubleday, *After the Plague*, 138.
75. Doubleday, *After the Plague*, 138.
76. Dorsey Armstrong, *Black Death*, 41.
77. Boccaccio, *Decameron*, preface.

Though death was abundantly prevalent and often abrupt, its arrival via the plague was arranged through God, whose provoked anger and desire for justice must be appeased.

William Langland's (1332–86) *Piers Plowman* contains a sequence of twenty-two dream visions from the late fourteenth century (ca. 1370–90). Langland's poem is an exploration of Christian faith for the narrator, "Will," and pursues how to live a good, Christian life. Commenting on the plague, Langland regards it as a divine warning, intended to provide moral correction of sinful people living in a corrupt society. So, the plague is viewed as a sacred punishment: Human sin has provoked God's anger, and human unrighteousness deserves to be penalized.[78]

It should be also mentioned that medieval art, too, visually depicts the plague as divine punishment. For example, in Dante's *Divine Comedy* (written ca. 1308–20), one illumination by Priamo della Quercia (1426–67) and Giovanni di Paolo di Grazia (ca. 1403–82) shows Dante (1265–1321) and Virgil (70 BCE–19 BCE) witnessing a group of sinners suffering the pain of plague in hell as punishment befitting the crime of human sin.[79]

Geoffrey Chaucer (ca. 1340–1400) was not able to finish *The Canterbury Tales* (which he began in 1386 or 1387), but his intention was "that each of some thirty pilgrims should tell two tales on the way [from London] to Canterbury and two on the way back."[80] He set the seventh tale, "The Pardoner's Tale" (a "pardoner" was one who had authority from the pope to sell pardons and indulgences), in the context of constant death from the plague. In this story, three companions become upset with all the deaths that are occurring. Personalizing "Death," they plan to find "him" and kill him. An inquiry is made of a poor, old man of Death's whereabouts, and the three arrive at the location the man specifies. But Death is not found there, but instead, a pile of gold coins. Each person plots how to grab all the gold for himself. One companion, the youngest of the three, goes to town to procure food and wine so they can stand watch over the gold coins until nightfall when they could transport the coins undetected; the other two conspire to kill him upon his return. However, the grocery shopper poisons two of the three bottles of wine with which he returns. He is killed by the other two, who afterward drink their bottles of wine and are themselves killed. Death has been found.

78. Langland, *Piers Plowman*.
79. Public Domain Review, "15th-Century Illuminations."
80. Chaucer, *Canterbury Tales*, 13.

As is the case with each tale, "The Pardoner's Tale" teaches some moral virtue to be upheld: This tale criticizes "greed" and "avarice." In the "Prologue" to the "Tale," Chaucer writes in the voice of a priest,

> But let me briefly make my purpose plain;
> I preach for nothing but for greed of gain.
> And use the same old text, as bold as brass,
> *Radix malorum est cupiditas* ["the root of evil is desire"].
> And thus I preach against the very vice
> I make my living out of—avarice.
> And yet however guilty of that sin
> Myself, with others I have power to win
> Them from it, I can bring them to repent;
> But that is not my principal intent.
> Covetousness is both the root and stuff
> Of all I preach. That ought to be enough.[81]

The "Tale" then proceeds to reference lust, gluttony, drunkenness, lechery, gambling, and false swearing to obey an oath, before homing in on the story of the three companions, who, sitting in a tavern having a drink, witness a funeral processional of a friend ("Death killed a thousand in the present plague") and make a pact to locate Death and destroy it.

Chaucer also wrote *The Book of the Duchess*, occasioned by the 1369 death from plague of the Duchess of Lancaster. In response to her death, Chaucer composed a dream vision poem, in which a knight tells the dreamer that he has lost his lady, "White," because he played "a game of chess with Fortune, and Fortune beat him and took his queen" (the name "White" is a play on the Duchess's name, "Blanche").[82] The dreamer then realizes that this is not a chess game at all, but real life and death and so he is compelled to commit the dream to verse.

Daniel Defoe (1660–1731)—well-known for his most famous novel, *Robinson Crusoe*—also wrote a *Journal of the Plague Year*, that year being 1665 and the location being London. First published in 1722 and set two hundred years after the major plague of the fourteenth century, these fictionalized remarks by a narrator (whose occupation is a saddler in the Whitechapel district of East London) set forward as historical facts, paint

---

81. Chaucer, *Canterbury Tales*, 199.
82. Dorsey Armstrong, *Black Death*, 143.

a picture similar to centuries before, with an onslaught of a disease that persons still did not understand and still could not mitigate. The rich still fled London, the poor still bore the brunt of deaths caused by plague, magistrates were still struggling to quarantine houses where infection had occurred, astrology and superstition still abounded. Though the narrator could have exited London, he decided to stay "and trust God with [his] safety and health," as "nothing descended upon us without the direction or the permission of Divine Power." As a result, he believed that if he fled the city, it would be "a kind of flying from God, and that He could cause His justice to overtake me when and where He thought fit." He reminisced that his brother, a merchant who had had experience among "Turks and Mahometans [Muslims] in Asia," said that these persons

> professed predestinating notions, and of every man's end being predetermined and unalterably beforehand decreed . . . they would go unconcerned into infected places and converse with infected persons, by which means they died at the rate of ten or fifteen thousand a week, whereas the Europeans or Christian merchants, who kept themselves retired and reserved, generally escaped the contagion.[83]

The narrator flirts with the idea of leaving, but having read the ninety-first psalm, verses 2–10, decides to remain:

> [I] will say to the Lord, "My refuge and my fortress; my God, in whom I trust." For he will deliver you from the snare of the fowler and from the deadly pestilence; he will cover you with his pinions, and under his wings you will find refuge; his faithfulness is a shield and buckler. You will not fear the terror of the night, or the arrow that flies by day, or the pestilence that stalks in darkness, or the destruction that wastes at noonday. A thousand may fall at your side, ten thousand at our right hand, but it will not come near you. You will only look with your eyes and see the punishment of the wicked. Because you have made the Lord your refuge, the Most High your dwelling place, no evil shall befall you, no scourge come near your tent.[84]

He later reflected that subsequent waves of the plague were indications that "God had not yet sufficiently scourged the city." "The great and dreadful God" was a mantra preached by some in the streets, astrologers made a

---

83. Defoe, *Journal*.
84. Defoe, *Journal*.

causal connection with a comet that preceded the outbreak of the plague, and old women saw visions and interpreted the dreams of others. The narrator stated, "It pleased God that I was still spared" though "100,000 souls were swept away."[85]

Muslims, too, believed that the plague was the result of God's will. But in Islam, the plague was also partially viewed as a gift or "blessing" from God which bestowed martyrdom on the Muslim victims who remained faithful and transported them instantly to paradise: "The plague is for [us] Muslims a martyrdom and a reward."[86] The Arab Muslim historian Ibn al-Wardi (1290–1349) describes in detail the advance of the plague, from China to India to Persia to the Crimea to Cyprus to Cairo to Alexandria (where only seven of seventy men were left alive) to upper Egypt to Gaza to Acre to Jerusalem to Damascus to Aleppo (where al-Wardi himself would succumb to the plague). Theologically acknowledging that the plague is acting by God's command and assaults wherever and whomever God decides, he prays, "Save us for [Muhammed's] sake from the attacks of the plague and give us shelter." He then asks God for forgiveness, for "the plague is surely part of His punishment."[87] Though the plague provided punishment and blessing for Muslims, it was a retribution alone to non-believers: "The plague is . . . for the disbelievers a punishment and a rebuke."[88]

The Plague of Emmaus (Amwas) afflicted Syria in 638–639 CE, and scholars conclude it was likely a reemergence of the mid-sixth century CE Plague of Justinian. The plague killed 25,000 Muslim soldiers and their relatives.[89] The experience of plague in the Muslim world is a reminder that the plague struck globally: It impacted the Middle East, the whole of Asia, and a major portion of Africa.[90] Since the Muslim world was thriving cultural, intellectually, and economically, and at a higher level than Europe, the devastation wrought by the plague was even more catastrophic.

There was also the view in the Islamic world that the disease was simply another trial to endure, such as a famine or a flood. This trial was also a "test": Would the severity and longevity of the plague be sufficient to cause

---

85. Defoe, *Journal*.
86. Al-Wardi, "Essay on the Report," 447–54.
87. Al-Wardi, "Essay on the Report," 447–54.
88. Al-Wardi, "Essay on the Report," 447–54.
89. Conrad, "Plague in the Early Medieval"; Dols, "Plague in Early Islamic History," 371–388.
90. Doubleday, *After the Plague*, 243.

one to lose faith? Or would that person persevere, retain religious conviction, and thereby "pass the test"? "When the Muslim endures misfortune, then patience is his worship."[91]

This notion of "test" in Islam is also the lesson in Chaucer's "The Clerk's Tale" in *The Canterbury Tales*: Griselda stoically and patiently perseveres through a deceptive set of dire experiences created by her husband, the Lord or Marquis of Saluzzo, Walter. In the end, the deception is revealed, and Griselda's constancy in the face of grief and suffering is rewarded by living happily ever after.[92] This tale is taken from both Boccaccio's *Decameron* and Petrarch, and the message from "The Clerk's Tale" is that we humans are often tested by God with difficulties, misfortunes, and agonies. But we must be resilient in our faith and thereby "pass the test."

Islam also admonished that one should not enter or flee plague-stricken regions, but instead should remain in place. The plague was not viewed to be contagious, because it came directly from God to specific individuals according to God's will and was not spread from person to person.[93] Muslims were also reminded of their obligation to care for the sick in areas that had been besieged by plague. In this, they were similar to the early church, which gained distinction in the Roman Empire by caring for victims of disease.[94]

Thus, both of these religious monotheisms—Christianity and Islam—regarded the plague as God's doing. God was in absolute control of everything that happened, so the plague must be ultimately attributable to God. God was punishing sinful humankind for its numerous sins, either by directly sending the plague or by indirectly working through natural or cosmic means to accomplish divine will. If natural means, then this was no different than Sodom and Gomorrah being punished by "fire and

---

91. Al-Wardi, "Essay on the Report," 447–54.

92. See the book of Job in the Hebrew Bible.

93. Two notable exceptions to this were Ibn Khatima and al-Khatib, who believed that the plague *was* contagious and that "to ignore science was an affront to God." However, the latter person was exiled from Granada to Morocco for clinging to and promoting this theory of contagion; Doubleday, *After the Plague*, 256.

94. Rodney Stark has written about the early church belief that, because God loves humans, and if so vice versa, then humans must show their love for God by loving one another. This included caring compassionately for others in times of sickness, distress, and oppression. This care was not to be restricted to members of the Christian community alone, but to *anyone* who needed help. Stark argues somewhat controversially that it was this that was primarily responsible for the growth of the early Christian church; *Rise of Christianity*, esp. ch. 4, "Epidemics, Networks, and Conversion."

brimstone." If cosmic means, then the devil may have temporary and limited power to orchestrate the plague, but God is more powerful (the cosmic struggle is "asymmetrical"—unbalanced—in favor of God) and therefore in the end in charge. While for both Christians and Muslims, the plague might be interpreted as a trial or a test (will a person give-up his or her faith in the face of such horror and suffering?), for Muslims it is also a "gift" or "blessing," for those who die still holding onto their faith are seen as martyrs who have a special place and reward in Paradise.

Chapter Two

The Spanish Flu

As medieval specialist Dorsey Armstrong has noted, the Spanish flu caused more deaths than the Black Death, but the latter killed half of the population of Europe. So, proportionately, the bubonic plague was more devastating—50 percent of the population compared to 2.5 percent.[1]

Yet the Spanish flu was, indeed, catastrophic: It erupted quite abruptly in 1918, spread very rapidly, and lasted until 1920. At least forty million persons died worldwide;[2] some argue "at least fifty million";[3] and a BBC documentary specifies fifty to one hundred million killed from 1918 to 1919.[4] Historian Alfred Crosby (1931–2018) remarks that one indisputable fact is that the Spanish flu virus "killed more humans than any other disease in a period of similar duration in the history of the world."[5] Gina Kolata, in her comprehensive and insightful study of the Spanish flu, notes that this epidemic killed "more Americans in a single year than died in battle in World War I, World War II, the Korean War, and the Vietnam War."[6] In fact, "ten times as many Americans died of the 1918 flu as from

---

1. Dorsey Armstrong, *Black Death*, 88; Barry, *Great Influenza*, 4.
2. Kolata, *Flu*.
3. Spinney, *Pale Rider*.
4. BBC, "Pandemic," featuring Professor John Oxford.
5. Crosby, *America's Forgotten Pandemic*, quoted in Kolata, *Flu*, 7.
6. Kolata, *Flu*, ix–x.

the First World War."[7] The world population in 1918 was 1.8 billion, and the United States population was 103 million of that number. Twenty-eight percent (or 28,840,000 persons) of the US population became ill, and 675,000 of them died.[8]

But perhaps the Spanish flu could be better and more accurately known as the "Kansas flu" or the "Boston flu." It was called the "Spanish flu" because Spain had remained neutral in the Great War and therefore reported forthrightly the deaths that were caused by the flu; other nations that participated in the war were reluctant to divulge such information because it could expose vulnerability and be interpreted as weakness, so they censored the news.[9]

> The Spanish flu [erupted in] the United States in March of 1918, which was the first of three waves between 1918 and 1919, with a possible fourth wave that lasted into 1920. The second wave, which began the fall of 1918, was the deadliest.[10]

The Spanish flu hit Kansas in early March 1918, at Camp Funston on the Fort Riley military reservation near Junction City.[11] Albert Gitchell, the company cook, reported to the infirmary complaining of a severe cold. By noon, the camp doctor had one hundred men to treat, all suffering from the same malady; this spread quickly to over five hundred soldiers.[12] Similar outbreaks occurred soon thereafter at other US military bases. By July, the first wave of the Spanish flu had spread globally, first hitting France in April; then England, China, and Japan in June. Large parts of Africa, South America, and Canada were somehow spared; and then the virus seemed to disappear.[13]

But the flu returned vengefully in a second wave in late August and the fall of 1918: A group of sailors in transit were docked in Boston, and by early September nearly 120 sailors were ill. At the same time, the flu hit Fort

---

7. McHugh, "How the 1918 Pandemic."

8. Linder and Grove, *Vital Statistics Rates*; cf. Kolata, *Flu*, 7.

9. Trimbee, "Spread of the Spanish Flu." Similarly, COVID-19 was regarded by some as the "China Virus" or the "Wuhan Virus" or "Chinese flu" or "Kung flu."

10. Breitzer, "American Religion and the Pandemic," transcript, 5.

11. PBS, "First Wave." Known also as "Three Day Fever" and "Purple Death," the Spanish Flu is believed to have most likely originated in the United States from an aviary source—domestic and wild birds (Hoag, "Study Revives Bird Origin").

12. PBS, "First Wave," 1.

13. Kolata, *Flu*, 11–12.

Devens northwest of Boston. Colonel Victor C. Vaughan, former president of the American Medical Association, who, along with three other doctors, visited the fort in the fall of 1918, had this to say about the situation:

> Hundreds of stalwart young men in the uniform of their country [come] into the wards of the hospital in groups of ten or more. They are placed on the cots until every bed is full, yet others crowd in. Their faces soon wear a bluish cast; a distressing cough brings up the blood-stained sputum. In the morning the dead bodies are stacked about the morgue like cord wood.[14]

Alfred Crosby, mentioned previously, who wrote the "first, major critical history" of the Spanish flu, called the disease "America's forgotten pandemic."[15] Apparently, the epidemic was so dreadful and so subsumed under all the horrors of the First World War that people did not want to talk about it, write about it, or remember it. The "War to end all wars" had been such an extensive and shocking nightmare, with twenty million deaths (including ten million civilians) and twenty-one million wounded,[16] that the Spanish flu was considered but one dimension of the tragedy. Indeed, Crosby found that encyclopedias granted sparse space to covering the Spanish flu: In the *Encyclopedia Britannica*, a total of three sentences was devoted to the Spanish flu; in the *Encyclopedia Americana*, but a single sentence.[17] Ironically,

> the Spanish influenza has stood out among modern pandemics until now, as the worst in recent times. In a way, it was the first truly global pandemic, thanks to comparably modern transportation and increased international interconnection.[18]

The religious responses to this "truly global pandemic" were multiple: While in ancient Greece, plagues were interpreted as originating from angry gods,[19] and while the majority religious opinion during the bubonic

---

14. Kolata, *Flu*, 16.
15. Crosby, *America's Forgotten Pandemic*, referenced in Kolata, *Flu*, 53.
16. Mougel, "World War I Casualties."
17. 115 Kolata, *Flu*, 52.
18. Breitzer, "American Religion and the Pandemic," 4.
19. For example, a riled-up Apollo, incensed by the insolence of ruler Agamemnon, started shooting his invisible plague arrows into mules, dogs, and then Greek soldiers. Homer, in the *Iliad*, said that the dead fell to the ground for nine days, and fires everywhere burned their bodies. The plague ended when Apollo was appeased by returning the priest Chryses's daughter (who had been captured in a raid by Agamemnon) and sacrificing one hundred cattle to Apollo (Kokkinidis, "Apollo vs. Agamemnon").

plague was a wrathful God whose righteousness and justice had demanded punishment, the greatest spiritual sentiment during the Spanish flu varied from being a punishment from God—e.g., for sin, or for worshiping science instead of God—to a tragic situation produced by natural causes, to a regression to *miasma* or "bad air" understandings of the past, to present conspiracy theories.

Orthodox Protestant Christianity stressed God's control of all events in the world—including such a plague as the Spanish flu—and indicated that sinful humanity was to blame for this pandemic. The "wrath of God" was responsible for meting out such severe justice for the transgressions of humanity. So, the Spanish flu plague must be a punishment for sin; for the world is "a world ruled by a God of justice."[20] Such direct expressions of God's anger were deserved by sinful humans, but it was also suggested that "divine intervention might utilize indirect means [such as a pandemic] to achieve its end."[21] So, regardless, things still happened in accordance with God's will and God's plan.

In Ireland, Spain, Portugal, and Latin America, Roman Catholic priests largely interpreted the Spanish flu pandemic as "a manifestation of divine anger at a range of personal and communal sins."[22] And religious leaders in England

> tended to see the epidemic as a manifestation of the wrath of God and a call for the people to turn to their faith for salvation. Some said God sent the epidemic to counter the "pride" and the "impotent boastings of modern science."[23]

Such a dogmatic belief in a punitive God as the sole source of the 1918 pandemic was echoed in other conservative Christian circles around the world too, "such as the Bible belts of the United States and the Netherlands, and in numerous evangelical congregations in North America, Europe, and its colonies."[24]

But if the Spanish flu was punishment, what was it specifically punishment *for*? There were many suggestions—the horrible war that claimed twenty million military and civilian deaths; exploitation of indigenous

---

20. Barry, *Great Influenza*, 44.
21. Phillips and Killingray, *Spanish Influenza Epidemic*, 7.
22. Phillips and Killingray, *Spanish Influenza Epidemic*; this is similar to the bubonic plague and the appeal to saints associated with epidemics/pandemics.
23. Kolata, *Flu*, 44, cf. 38.
24. Quinn, *Flu*, 142–43; Phillips and Killingray, *Spanish Influenza Epidemic*, 67.

peoples by Western imperialism and colonialism; moral degeneracy, as observed especially in the lower classes; greed and opulence in the upper classes; religious skepticism following the Enlightenment and scientific explanations, rather than religious ones, for prior natural events; pride in "worshiping" science as a "false god" and giving up on "the one true God and the one true Path" of Christian faith.[25]

One of Holland's premier, orthodox Protestant theologians and a former prime minister, Abraham Kuyper, protested that restricting churches from being able to gather for worship violated the respective roles of church and state and infringed on the freedom of religious conscience.[26] He went on to suggest that the Spanish flu was God's "rod of wrath," by which God was "punishing humankind for no longer fearing Him."[27] Kuyper was horrified that people trusted in science rather than in God.[28]

> Tellingly, the sins being punished included not only familiar moral, religious, and social transgressions, but also "worshipping science," which was epitomized by the medico-scientific explanations advanced to account for the Spanish flu. These [explanations] were classic examples of the vanity and conceit which arose when human beings thought they knew better than God and placed science above him.[29]

Appealing to the Ten Commandments, it was asserted that "God demanded that 'we should have no other gods before Him,' yet people had made science and materialism the very goal of their existence: 'It itself is their God.'"[30]

Orthodox Protestant theologian Gerard Wisse regarded the Spanish flu as a "wake-up call," designed to alert persons to their need to accept Christ now and be assured of eternal salvation, since no one knew who would live and who would die from the malady. In short, since the Spanish flu could end anyone's life, persons should be prepared to meet their

---

25. Spinney, *Pale Rider*, 79.

26. Krijger, "Coping with COVID-19," 3; this charge by Kuyper was echoed by the successful court case in New York City during COVID filed by three Jewish congregations and the Roman Catholic Archdiocese of Brooklyn protesting limitations on religious gatherings (Walsh, "U.S. Supreme Court Blocks").

27. Krijger, "Coping with COVID-19," 3.

28. Krijger, "Coping with COVID-19," 3.

29. Phillips and Killingray, *Spanish Influenza Epidemic*, 8.

30. Phillips, *Black October*, 140.

Maker. Although on the one hand, this meant that eternal damnation awaited anyone who died without professing Christ, it also meant that those who did accept Christ could die without fear, because they were assured of their salvation.[31]

And, like the time of the bubonic plague nearly six hundred years prior, some other orthodox Protestant preachers and theologians pointed to the Spanish flu as a clear indication that the end of time was at hand. Such a "devastating plague" was "an eschatological sign . . . of the herald of the Second Coming [of Christ and the end time]."[32] In fact, the Spanish flu was the "beginning of the affliction foretold in the Book of Revelation."[33] Much worse would follow, but simultaneously, Christians should rejoice because Jesus was returning soon, and the Last Judgment would finally occur.

Although this apocalyptic vision was largely absent in the thought of Roman Catholic theologians, some of these Catholic thinkers argued that the power of the celebration of the Mass and its Holy Eucharist would keep the Spanish flu away.[34] One Spanish bishop wrote that the cessation of the plague in his area was due to the fact that many persons continued to attend Mass despite the Spanish flu and government's advice to stay away and stay apart, and this placated "God's legitimate anger," and, as a result, God's mercy had lifted the pandemic.[35]

In addition, it was recommended that the intercessory power of saints could be tapped to ward off the disease and to release its stranglehold on the population. The same priests in Ireland, Spain, Portugal, and Latin America who saw the Spanish flu as an expression of God's anger over human sins also argued that the expiation of these sins could be aided by the intercession of saints associated with pestilence.[36] As in the time of the Black Death, St. Roch was one of the major figures to whom appeal was made. Beyond this, massive street processions were held, for example, all over the "Catholic South" in The Netherlands.[37] These features are reminiscent of those during the fourteenth-century bubonic plague.

---

31. Phillips, "Why Did It Happen?," 34.
32. Phillips, "Why Did It Happen?," 34.
33. Phillips, "Why Did It Happen?," 34.
34. This is similar to the proclamation in some Protestant churches during COVID-19 that "Jesus is my vaccine."
35. Phillips and Killingray, *Spanish Influenza Epidemic*, 7.
36. Phillips and Killingray, *Spanish Influenza Epidemic*, 7.
37. Phillips and Killingray, *Spanish Influenza Epidemic*, 5.

However, more progressive theologians rejected these points of view, saying instead that "God would never return evil for evil or that He did not directly intervene in the world."[38] Thus, at the other end of the theological spectrum were theologians and pastors who

> called on their congregants to take scientifically-based measures to prevent infection rather than just beseeching God "to perform a miracle in the preservation of health. Christians do not discount their faith in the omnipotence of their God by keeping their bodies and streets clean and non-germ producing, by using care in traffic and travel, accepting vaccination, sprays, and disinfectants, and keeping God's own laws of health and life."[39]

One Anglican bishop contended that God did not send the influenza because God was angry with us and set out to punish us.[40] Instead, what caused the Spanish flu was human neglect of conditions set down by God as necessary for human health, such as fresh air, cleanliness, and nourishment. When these conditions were ignored and replaced by foul air, dirt, poor and insufficient food, then humans who tolerated such opposite conditions were guilty before God and before humanity.[41]

Protestant pastor Francis James Grimke included in his November 3, 1918, sermon at the Fifteenth Street Presbyterian Church in Washington, DC, the following words:

> Our own beautiful city has suffered terribly, making it necessary, as a precautionary measure, to close the schools, theaters, churches, and to forbid all public gathering within doors as well as outdoors.... In a matter like this, it is always wise to submit to such restrictions for the time being. If, as a matter of fact, it was dangerous to meet in theaters and in the schools, it certainly was no less dangerous to meet in churches. The fact that the churches were places of religious gathering, and others not, would not affect in the least the health question involved. If avoiding crowds lessens the danger of being infected, it [is] wise to take the precaution and not needlessly run into danger, and expect God to protect us.[42]

---

38. Phillips and Killingray, *Spanish Influenza Epidemic*, 3.

39. Phillips and Killingray, *Spanish Influenza Epidemic*, 8; quote is from *Age-Herald*, Birmingham, AL, October 14, 1918.

40. *Church Chronicle*, November 28, 1918; cited in Phillips, *Black October*, 144.

41. *Church Chronicle*, November 28, 1918; cited in Phillips, *Black October*, 144.

42. Pellowe, "How the Church Responded."

However, he goes on in his sermon to affirm that God had a purpose behind the Spanish flu, whether God sent it or allowed it to be sent:

> I have been asking myself the question, what is the meaning of it all? What ought it to mean to us? Is it to come and go and we be no wiser, or better for it? Surely God had a purpose in it, and it is our duty to find out, as far as we may, what that purpose is, and try to profit by it.[43]

In other words, though he does not contend that God's purpose was explicitly to punish humans for their sins, it *was* God's will that the Spanish flu happened, either through direct causation or through divine permission. "God knows what He is doing . . . and great good is coming [out of it]."[44] So, according to his view, God's purpose may be unknown, but humans can and must struggle to comprehend that purpose and thereby benefit from that struggle and achieve perhaps partial comprehension. At any rate, "good" will result in the end.

During the Spanish flu pandemic, a number of major cities mandated quarantines and enacted social-distancing as public health measures—significantly among them St. Louis, Boston, and Richmond. Laws were passed requiring the wearing of masks in Seattle, Chicago, and San Francisco.[45] A pamphlet from October 1918, issued by the United States Public Health Service of the Treasury Department indicated that the Spanish flu was spread by droplets sprayed from nose and throat and advised covering coughs and sneezes with a handkerchief, avoiding crowds, walking to work if possible, not spitting on sidewalks, not using common drinking cups and towels, and, if one felt ill, going to bed and summoning a doctor.[46]

America's neighbor to the north, Canada, also imposed restrictions:

> [Since no medicine can prevent Spanish flu, persons are to] keep away from public meetings, theatres, and other places where crowds are assembled. Keep the mouth and nose covered while coughing or sneezing. When a member of the household becomes ill, place him in a room by himself. The room should be warm, but

---

43. Pellowe, "How the Church Responded."
44. Pellowe, "How the Church Responded."
45. Boyce and Katz, "1918 Influenza Pandemic."
46. Boyce and Katz, "1918 Influenza Pandemic," para. 8, referencing a US Public Health Service public education campaign, Oct. 1918, Library of Congress, Rare Book and Special Collections Division.

well ventilated. The attendant should put on a mask before entering the room of those ill of the disease.[47]

In terms of church and other closures, a public notice in Kingston, Ontario, stated that, upon the authority of the Board of Health and the Office of the Mayor,

> after Oct. 16th [1918], and until further notice,
>
> 1. Theatres and Moving Picture Houses shall be closed and remain closed
> 2. Churches and Chapels of all denominations shall be closed and remain closed on Sundays.
> 3. All Schools, Public or Private, including Sunday Schools, shall close and remain closed.
> 4. Hospitals shall be closed to visitors.
> 5. No public shall be admitted to courts, except those essential to the prosecution of the cases called.
> 6. . . . the public . . . [will not] crowd into street cars and [will] avoid as much as possible any crowded train or an assembly of any kind. . . . every case of illness should send in a call to a physician.[48]

British Columbia, likewise, issued a similar public notice:

> In order to prevent the spread of Spanish Influenza, all Schools, public and private, Churches, Theatres, Moving Picture Halls, Pool Rooms and other places of amusement, and Lodge meetings, are to be closed until further notice. All public gatherings consisting of ten or more are prohibited. [signed by the Mayor and dated October 19, 1918].[49]

Most religious bodies followed state-ordered restrictions, while some religious bodies opposed them. And as many churches closed their doors, they found ways to continue ministry and pastoral care to their flocks: For example, sermons were printed in newspapers (since, of course, technologies such as Zoom and Facebook were decades away in the future). And the clergy were mostly supportive of public health measures that had closed the

---

47. A 1918 Alberta, Canada, poster, in Pellowe, "How the Church Responded."
48. A 1918 Ontario, Canada, poster, in Pellowe, "How the Church Responded."
49. A 1918 British Columbia, Canada, poster, in Pellowe, "How the Church Responded."

churches as well as other places of public gathering. Although there were some instances of defiance, most churches acted in compliance.[50]

It has been noted that in the midst of the stark realities of the Spanish flu, the church performed charitable and compassionate actions to help out: Churches offered "space for the sick to relieve hospital overcrowding, [and] its members and functionaries [served] as volunteer nurses."[51] "When there were no doctors, missionaries, nuns, and other religious figures, laypersons took up the slack."[52] This was an echo from the second and third centuries CE, when the early church cared for the sick and buried the dead in the Antonine Plague (165–180 CE) and the Cyprian Plague (249–262 CE).[53] It has been acknowledged that, because most persons other than Christians had fled during those early plagues, Christian compassion and devotion were quite positive on the pagan world. As a result, the ancient church grew significantly.[54] Consistently, the time of the Spanish flu also manifested an increased respect for the church and its ministry.

The study "Religion and Science in Three Pandemics: 1817, 1918, and 2019" observes that there has often been a predominant "warfare model" in the relationship between religion and science.[55] Accordingly, faith-based explanations for catastrophes compete with science-based explanations for those same catastrophes. One point made by the study that is historically and theologically significant here is that when one of the disciplines fails to explain or grant remedy from a catastrophe, it is rejected for the time being and the other discipline is embraced. For example, during the fourteenth-century bubonic plague, the church fell under attack because it appeared powerless to do anything to stop the onslaught and to help its people. The faithful expected a theological response to the rapidity and the enormity of deaths because there was not a germ theory of disease to which to refer. However, more numerous and more fervent prayers did not work; nor did additional church services; nor did pilgrimages (which only increased the number of deaths due to closer physical proximity); some priests tended

50. Pellowe, "How the Church Responded," 7.
51. Breitzer, "American Religion and the Pandemic," 3.
52. Spinney, *Pale Rider*, 138.
53. Pellowe, "How the Church Responded," 7.
54. See Stark, *Rise of Christianity*, ch. 4.
55. Phillips, "Religion and Science," 435. It is noteworthy that this study defines religion as "faith or belief in a supernatural being ultimately determining all events" ("Religion and Science," 436). That definition reveals a particular and biased concept of divine power and God's providence that, though prevalent, is not exclusive.

their flocks, others fled to the hills because of concern for their own health and wellbeing; appeals to saints flourished; all to no avail![56]

And so, in the absence of scientific investigations and efficacious orthodox theological contributions, people turned to radical personal pietism, as expressed for example in the flagellants' movement, superstition (bizarre "remedies" such as drinking urine, breathing in the nauseous smells of latrines, wearing trinkets that were fervently hoped to ward off the disease, etc.), and scapegoating minority communities such as Jews.

But now, in the time of the twentieth-century influenza epidemic, when science, which had seemed invincible with its banner of germ theory of disease before the onset of the Spanish flu, failed to address human fear and suffering and alleviate them, the optimism it engendered in the general public was eroded, and persons turned to faith responses. During the early twentieth-century influenza pandemic, science appeared powerless to do anything to thwart the disease and to prevent rapid death (Spanish flu was sometimes called the "Three-Day Fever" because that's sometimes how long persons lived after they contracted it). It especially impacted young persons between the ages of twenty and forty, normally those least likely to be attacked, since most diseases assault the very young and the very old.[57]

Prior to the Spanish flu, science, which had unleashed its power to observe, to experiment, and to eradicate a number of diseases, had been seen as the champion of the people. Diseases such as cholera, tuberculosis, malaria, and yellow fever—long afflicting the human race—had been eradicated. In the fifty years preceding the outbreak of the Spanish flu, the revolutionary "germ theory of disease" had enabled science to identify pathogens and then seek to curtail them. In his 1840 essay "On Miasmata and Contagia," German physician and pathologist Friedrich Gustav Jakob Henle first formulated the earliest modern germ theory of disease.[58] As a result, "every eighteen months, a new pathogen was identified, and it went on for years," Alfred Crosby noted.[59] "Each discovery drove home the message that science was conquering disease."[60] By the early twentieth century,

---

56. See Zentner, "Black Death and Its Impact"; Doubleday, *After the Plague*, 198–207; Dorsey Armstrong, *Black Death*, 113–19.

57. Boyce and Katz, "1918 Influenza Pandemic."

58. Barry, *Great Influenza*, 51.

59. Quoted in Kolata, *Flu*, 54.

60. Kolata, *Flu*, 54.

many Americans had lulled themselves into thinking that the wonders of medical science could vanquish any foe, no matter how microscopic.... The memory of a world stalked by infectious disease had dimmed. People [became] complacent, almost smug, about disease and death.[61]

In the same time period, it was reported by *Ladies Home Journal* magazine that the parlor of homes, customarily used for viewing deceased family members, was to become known now as the "living room," not a place for the dead.[62]

But now, with the devastating impact of the Spanish flu, science could offer no effective vaccine, no miracle pill to swallow, no magic elixir to gargle. The Spanish flu was "confounding even the most brilliant medical minds of the time [so] fear set in."[63] "The flu epidemic... made a mockery of the newfound optimism."[64] Science had nothing to prescribe and no preventative to administer. Doctors prescribed anything from "the wonder drug" aspirin, to quinine, to arsenic preparations, to castor oil, to iodine, to bloodletting, to alcohol in small doses (it should be noted that this was the age of prohibition), to cigarette smoke, to mercury vapor, to mustard poultices, to sugar lumps soaked in kerosene, to fires of aromatic plants burned twice daily in front of persons' houses (to clear the *miasma* or "bad air"), to tonics such as the popular "Dr. Kilmer's Swamp-Root."[65] None of these "remedies" was effective. "The mystery of the 1918 flu was beyond the powers of science and medicine to solve."[66] As a result, "there was a definite feeling that science had failed us."[67]

In addition, suspicion accompanied fear of the disease and the sense of scientific failure, and consequently, conspiracy theories emerged: When the second wave struck Boston in the fall of 1918, speculation arose that German U-boats had entered the harbor and disseminated influenza-spouting germs. Or, alternately, those U-boats had put ashore German soldiers who planted the seeds of disease in public places such as theaters, restaurants, cinemas, and churches. Or, perhaps the Germans had

---

61. Kolata, *Flu*, 48.
62. Kolata, *Flu*, 48.
63. PBS, "Placing Blame," 1.
64. Kolata, *Flu*, 54.
65. Spinney, *Pale Rider*, 122–25.
66. Kolata, *Flu*, 65.
67. McHugh, "How the 1918 Pandemic."

inserted the flu into aspirin made by the German drug company Bayer, founded in 1863 and whose production of dyes and pharmaceuticals was commonly known to have been altered by the government into explosives and chemicals in World War I.[68]

Credence was given to these conspiracy theories by the pronouncements of some public officials, one of them being Lt. Col. Philip Doan, head of the Health and Sanitation Section of the Emergency Fleet Corporation, who, on September 17, 1918, voiced his opinion that

> it would be quite easy for one of these German agents to turn loose influenza germs in a theater or some other place where large numbers of persons are assembled. The Germans have started epidemics in Europe, and there is no reason why they should be particularly gentle with America.[69]

Other popular opinions pointed to causes such as poisonous gas drifting over the Atlantic from the trenches on the Western front, vapors from decomposing bodies and exploding munitions in the war, coal dust, animal distemper from dogs and cats, and even dirty dishwater.[70]

Unfortunately, but perhaps inevitably, bigotry toward immigrants and minority groups escalated: As reporter Jess McHugh put it, "The ravages of a pandemic only bring simmering societal issues to a boil, underscoring the prejudices that already exist."[71] Despite the Kansas source of the Spanish flu, and since Americans believed themselves to be "only victims," others must have been to blame. Fingers pointed in an easterly direction, not only to immigrants from Asia, but also to natives of the Far East. In its most extreme form,

> this xenophobia manifested itself in accusations that Asians were to blame [not only for the Spanish flu, but also] for falling birth rates in Europe, rising criminality, the kidnapping of women for the white slave trade, and even vampires (who were supposed to have reached Transylvania from China via the Silk Road).[72]

---

68. Spinney, *Pale Rider*, 76.

69. PBS, "Placing Blame," 2; Spinney, *Pale Rider*, 76.

70. More recent research has demonstrated that the Spanish flu virus came from North American domestic and wild birds, rather than from a mixture of swine and human viruses (and certainly not from a conspiracy theory concerning Germany), as suspected before; Worobey et al., "Synchronized Global Sweep," 254–57.

71. McHugh, "How the 1918 Pandemic."

72. Spinney, *Pale Rider*, 153; cf. Witchard, *England's Yellow Peril*. "Scapegoating," of

When science and conspiracy theories and popular opinions seemed finally and ultimately impotent to decipher and curb the Spanish flu, religious interpretations and appeals returned to center stage:

> In 1918, when a more mystical, pre-Darwinian era was still in living memory, and four years of war had worn down people's psychological defenses, it was even easier for them to fall back on the belief that epidemics were acts of God. They looked for and found evidence to confirm them in that belief.[73]

In summary, then, the Spanish flu was primarily, though not exclusively, seen religiously as an "act of God," most likely a punishment, a corrective, a test, or a malady surrounded in divine mystery. Regardless of which, but assuredly, God was in complete control, God's will was perfectly just, and God's inscrutable divine plan would eventually work through everything for a good goal or outcome.

---

course, was one of the responses made during the fourteenth-century bubonic plague when Christians blamed Jews for the pandemic; it was also a response made during COVID-19 when China was blamed for spreading the coronavirus.

73. Spinney, *Pale Rider*, 78.

Chapter Three

COVID-19

COVID-19 (SEVERE, ACUTE RESPIRATORY syndrome coronavirus 2 [SARS-CoV-2]) emerged at the end of 2019 in China. There were two competing theories as to how the virus developed and then spread: One perspective was that it resulted from a laboratory accident at the Wuhan Institute of Virology (WIV), an "overspill."[1] The other was that it originated in a bat species known for harboring coronaviruses. The consensus now seems to be the second explanation, that it originated in wild bats—the thumb-sized intermediate horseshoe bat—and was communicated to humans through a wildlife host. The coronavirus was not harmful to those wild bats, but was so to other species, including humans. It has been concluded that the live wildlife trade in the Huanan Seafood Wholesale Market in the city of Wuhan, China, communicated the virus to humans.[2]

Indeed, a joint study conducted in early 2021 by the People's Republic of China and the World Health Organization indicated that the virus descended from a coronavirus that infects wild bats and likely spread to humans through intermediary wildlife.[3] According to articles published in July 2022 in *Science*, the transmission of the virus into humans occurred

---

1. Gostin and Gronvall, "Origins of COVID-19," 2305–8.

2. Pekar, "Molecular Epidemiology," 960–66; Jiang and Wang, "Wildlife Trade Is Likely," 925–26.

3. World Health Organization, *WHO-Convened Global Study*.

through two "spillover" events in November 2019 and was likely due to live wildlife trade.[4]

This is "zoonotic spillover," rather than "spillover" from a laboratory. It should be noted that the laboratory source theory was one of the earliest suggestions, sometimes combined with a sinister note of conspiracy intentions by the Chinese:

> A minority of scientists and some members of the U.S. intelligence community believe the virus may have been unintentionally leaked from a laboratory such as the Wuhan Institute of Virology. The U.S. intelligence community has mixed views on the issue, but overall agrees with the scientific consensus that the virus was not developed as a biological weapon and is unlikely to have been genetically engineered. There is no evidence SARS-CoV-2 existed in any laboratory prior to the pandemic.[5]

As noted in previous chapters, conspiracy theories also characterized the bubonic plague (e.g., Jews and/or other "undesirables" poisoned wells) and the Spanish flu (e.g., German infiltrators penetrated American borders and dispensed germs in theaters, churches, and other crowded venues).

The first confirmed human infections were in Wuhan. A study of the first 41 cases of confirmed COVID-19, published in January 2020 in the international medical journal *The Lancet* (founded 1823), reported the earliest date of onset of symptoms as December 1, 2019.[6] Official publications from the World Health Organization reported the earliest onset of symptoms as December 8, 2019.[7] Human-to-human transmission was confirmed by the World Health Organization and Chinese authorities by January 20, 2020.[8]

In December 2019, the spread of the infection was almost entirely driven by human-to-human transmission.[9] The number of COVID-19 cases in Wuhan gradually increased, reaching 60 by December 20,[10] and

---

4. Pekar, "Molecular Epidemiology," 960–66; Gill, "Covid Origin Studies"; Worobey et al., "Huanan Seafood Whole Market," 951–59.

5. Hao et al., "Origins of COVID-19 Pandemic."

6. As mentioned in Wu et al., "Outbreak of COVID-19," 217–20.

7. World Health Organization, "Novel Coronavirus—China."

8. Kessler, "Trump's False Claim."

9. *China CDC Weekly*, "Epidemiological Characteristics," 113–22; Heymann and Shindo, "Covid-19," 542–45.

10. Bryner, "First Known Case of Coronavirus."

at least 266 by December 31.[11] On December 24, a fluid sample from the lungs of an unresolved clinical case was sent for analysis to the Vision Medicals Company in Guangzhou. Three days later, Vision Medicals informed the Wuhan Central Hospital and the Chinese Center for Disease Control and Prevention (established 2002) of the results of the test, showing a new coronavirus.[12]

During the early stages of the outbreak, the number of cases doubled approximately every seven and a half days.[13] In early and mid-January 2020, the virus spread to other Chinese provinces, helped by the Chinese New Year migration and Wuhan being a transport hub and major rail interchange.[14] On January 20, China reported nearly 140 new cases in one day, including two people in Beijing and one in Shenzhen, 1,353 miles from Beijing.[15] Later official data show 6,174 people had already developed symptoms by then,[16] and more may have been infected. A report in *The Lancet* on January 24 indicated human transmission and strongly recommended personal protective equipment for health workers and advocated that testing for the virus was essential due to its "pandemic potential."[17]

In the initial year, COVID-19 infected ninety-six million people and killed two million. Four hundred thousand of those infections were in the United States.[18]

COVID-19 sneaked in as a surprise. Would it be like SARS, which was threatening but ultimately contained? It first became a topic of conversation in the United States in January of 2020 when the Centers for Disease Control and Prevention (CDC) alerted the nation to the outbreak abroad.[19] On January 20, 2020, the first case was reported in the state of Washington, a thirty-year-old man from Snohomish County who had recently returned from Wuhan, China. The World Health Organization (WHO) declared COVID-19 a pandemic in March 2020.

---

11. Thomson, "Birth of a Pandemic."
12. Yuding et al., "Tracing the Coronavirus's Origins"; and Yu et al., "How Early Signs."
13. Li et al., "Early Transmission Dynamics," 1199–207.
14. World Health Organization, "Report of the WHO-China Joint Mission."
15. News Wires, "China Confirms Sharp Rise."
16. *China CDC Weekly*, "Epidemiological Characteristics," 113–22.
17. Huang et al., "Clinical Features of Patients Infected," 497–506.
18. Weise and Weintraub, "Where Did COVID-19 Come From?"
19. Northwestern Medicine, "COVID-19 Pandemic Timeline."

COVID demonstrated itself to be both fast-paced—highly contagious—and pathogenic—highly virulent. As a result, COVID-19 became termed "the greatest health crisis of our time."[20]

Unlike the Spanish flu, which impacted most greatly young persons from ages twenty to forty, COVID struck most lethally at the elderly. Three years after the beginning of the pandemic in the United States, "Americans 70 and up were being admitted with COVID at a rate four times higher than that of the general population, with most fatalities among people over 64."[21]

As a virus, COVID-19 mutated multiple times: As of December 2021, there were five dominant variants of SARS-CoV-2 spreading among global populations—the Alpha variant (B.1.1.7, formerly called the UK variant), first found in London and Kent, the Beta variant (B.1.351, formerly called the South Africa variant), the Gamma variant (P.1, formerly called the Brazil variant), the Delta variant (B.1.617.2, formerly called the India variant),[22] and the Omicron variant (B.1.1.529), which had spread to fifty-seven countries as of December 7, 2021.[23]

And in the summer of 2023, a new variant emerged: "Now [in 2023] the dominant strain circulating in the United States" is EG.5, also known as "Eris."[24] So, there was a sixth variant, with a number of subvariants within each of those variants. In April 2024, a group of new virus strains known as the FLiRT variants (based on the technical names of their two mutations) began to spread, followed in June by a variant known as LB.1. The FLiRT strains are subvariants of Omicron, and together they accounted for the majority of COVID cases in the United States at the beginning of July 2024.

The following timeline provides information about selected moments in the COVID-19 pandemic in the United States and around the world beginning from its known origins in late 2019 to August 2023.[25]

On January 13, 2020, the Thailand Ministry of Public Health confirmed the first laboratory-confirmed case of the SARS-CoV-2 virus outside

---

20. Hochman, "Three Years In," 8.

21. Hochman, "Three Years In," 8.

22. Centers for Disease Control and Prevention, "New COVID-19 Variants."

23. World Health Organization, "Weekly Epidemiological Update"; World Health Organization, "Classification of Omicron (B.1.1.529)."

24. Kee, "What to Know About Eris."

25. Edited, abridged, and expanded from the Centers for Disease Control and Prevention, "CDC Museum COVID-19 Timeline," December 12, 2019–July 8, 2022.

of China. The same was discovered in Japan on January 15. On January 19, China had 278 cases, while South Korea revealed 1 case.

On January 20, the US had its first case, reported in Washington State. Four days later, there was a case in Illinois. Two days following, two cases were confirmed in Arizona and California, bringing the total to five. At the end of the month the virus spread between two persons in Illinois, the first case of inter-person transmission not due to travel. Total cases now equaled seven.

On February 10, 2020, worldwide deaths from COVID-19 reached 1,013. The next day, the World Health Organization announced the official name for the disease, "COVID-19." On February 23, Italy locked down the country due to its being a "global COVID-19 hotspot." Two days later, the CDC warned that there would need to be serious mitigation efforts such as school closings, workplace shutdowns, and the canceling of large gatherings and public events, stating that the "disruption to everyday life may be severe."

On March 3, 2020, the CDC reported 60 cases of COVID-19 across Arizona, California, Florida, Georgia, Illinois, Massachusetts, New Hampshire, New York, Oregon, Rhode Island, Washington, and Wisconsin. Of the 60 COVID-19 infections detected, 21 were travel-related, 11 were from person-to-person spread, and 27 were unknown. On March 11, 2020, after more than 118,000 cases in 114 countries and 4,291 deaths, the World Health Organization declared COVID-19 a pandemic. Two days afterward, the Trump administration declared a nationwide emergency and issued an additional travel ban on non-US citizens traveling from 26 European countries due to COVID-19. The following day, the CDC issued a "no sail order" for all cruise ships, calling for them to cease activity in all waters over which the US held jurisdiction.

In mid-March 2020, states began to implement shutdowns in order to prevent the spread of COVID-19. The New York City public school system—the largest school system in the US with 1.1 million students—shut down, while Ohio called for restaurants and bars to close. On March 17, Moderna began the first human trials of a vaccine to protect against COVID-19 at a research facility in Seattle, Washington, while the University of Minnesota launched a clinical trial testing of hydroxychloroquine, an FDA-approved drug for the prevention and treatment of malaria, as a possible treatment of COVID-19. Two days later, California Governor Gavin Newsom issued a statewide stay-at-home order to slow the spread of COVID-19 instructing residents to only leave their homes when necessary and shutting down all but essential businesses. Toward the end of the month, on March 27, 2020, the Trump administration signed the Coronavirus Aid, Relief, and Economic Security (CARES) Act into law. The act included funding for 1,200 dollars per adult (with enlarged payments for families with children), expanded unemployment benefits, forgivable small business loans, loans to major industries and corporations, and expanded funding to state and local governments in response to the economic crisis caused by COVID-19.

On March 30, 2020, the Centers for Disease Control and Prevention issued a domestic travel advisory for New York, New Jersey, and Connecticut due to high community transmission of COVID-19 in those states, urging residents to refrain from all non-essential domestic travel for at least 14 days, effective immediately. On the last day of the month, Dr. Anthony Fauci and Dr. Deborah Brix announced that between 100,000 and 240,000 deaths in the US were expected, even if social distancing and public health measures were perfectly enacted.

On April 3, 2020, the Centers for Disease Control and Prevention announced new mask-wearing guidelines and recommended that all people wear a mask when outside of the home. The following day, more than one million cases of COVID-19 were confirmed worldwide, a more than ten-fold increase in less than a month. On April 7, data from the Chicago Department of Public Health as reported by the *Chicago Tribune* showed that, despite being about 30 percent of the total population, Black people accounted for 68 percent of the COVID-19 related deaths in Chicago and were dying of COVID-19 at a rate nearly six-times greater than that of White Chicagoans, who accounted for 33 percent of the population and approximately 14 percent of the deaths. These numbers illuminated for many the racial disparities of the COVID-19 pandemic in the US.

Three days later, it was reported that the US was the country with the most reported COVID-19 cases and deaths: With over 18,600 deaths and more than 500,000 cases in under four months, the US had surpassed Italy and Spain as the global hotspot for the virus. With 159,937 confirmed cases, New York State now had more reported cases of COVID-19 than Spain (153,000), Italy (143,000), or China (82,000). Amid critical hospital bed and ventilator shortages, aerial images emerged of workers in hazardous material suits burying coffins in mass graves at Hart Island off the Bronx, an area used for over 150 years by New York City officials as a burial site for those with no next-of-kin or who could not afford funerals.

Mid-month, President Trump announced that the US would cease contributing funding to the World Health Organization, an action that shook the global public health community. On April 16, his administration released a plan that outlined how states should reopen, calling for states or metropolitan areas to meet benchmarks like reducing COVID-19 cases or deaths before reopening or stopping mitigation strategies (like required masking). Four days later, as the pandemic grew, awareness became acute of shortages of personal protective equipment (PPE) like gowns, eye shields, masks, and even body bags, particularly in New York. Slightly over a week later, the states of Georgia, Alaska, and Oklahoma began to partially reopen despite concerns from health experts saying it was too early to do so. On the last day of the month, the Trump administration launched Operation Warp Speed, an initiative to produce a vaccine against the SARS-CoV-2 virus as quickly as possible. The operation funded the development of six promising vaccine candidates while they were still in the clinical trial phase, including the Pfizer-BioNTech and Moderna mRNA vaccines.

On May 8, 2020, the Associated Press reported that top White House officials blocked a Centers for Disease Control and Prevention document, "Guidance for Implementing the Opening Up America Again Framework," that included detailed advice on how to safely reopen the country. The next day it was announced that the unemployment rate in the US was 14.7 percent, the highest since the Great Depression. With 20.5 million people out of work, the hospitality, leisure, and healthcare industries took the hardest hits overall, affecting essential workers, people with lower incomes, and racial and ethnic minority workers disproportionately. Mid-May, it was announced that the Navajo Nation now had the highest COVID-19 infection rate per capita in the US. But by the end of the month, through lockdown, curfew, staying at home, and masking, the Navajo Nation became a model for implementing a unified COVID-19 response. On May 28, it was revealed that the recorded death toll from COVID-19 in the US surpassed 100,000.

On June 8, 2020, the World Bank stated that the COVID-19 pandemic would plunge the global economy into the worst recession since World War II. Two days afterward, the number of confirmed COVID-19 cases in the US surpassed two million. Two weeks after this, the CDC noted that risk increases with age. And on the last day of the month, Dr. Anthony Fauci warned a Senate committee that the number of new COVID-19 cases in the

US could soon rise from 40,000 to 100,000 new infections every day, likely overwhelming an already burdened healthcare system.

On July 7, 2020, the number of confirmed COVID-19 cases in the US surpassed three million. Two days following, the World Health Organization announced that the SARS-CoV-2 virus that causes COVID-19 could be transmitted through the air and was likely being spread by asymptomatic individuals. In mid-July, the Centers for Disease Control and Prevention again called on all people to wear cloth face masks when leaving their homes to prevent the spread of COVID-19, calling masks "a critical tool in the fight against COVID-19." On the same day, it was reported that Florida, Texas, Oklahoma, Mississippi, North Carolina, South Carolina, and Georgia had both the greatest percentage of adults who were currently uninsured and the highest numbers of new COVID-19 cases. On July 16, many states, including California, Michigan, and Indiana, postponed re-opening plans as COVID-19 case numbers rose. It was also reported on the same date a record number of COVID-19 infections in a single day, with 75,600 new cases.

On August 4, 2020, a study found that more than 50 percent of all people living in rural areas in the US had no intensive care unit (ICU) beds available, while only 3 percent of the communities with higher incomes had no ICU beds. One week later, the Trump administration agreed to pay 1.5 billion dollars, or 15 dollars per dose, to Moderna for 100 million doses of a COVID-19 vaccine. Mid-August, the Centers for Disease Control and Prevention reported the results from a representative panel survey on mental health conducted among adults across the US in June of 2020: 41 percent of responders admitted to struggling with mental health, and 11 percent had seriously considered suicide recently. At the same time, COVID-19 became the third leading cause of death in the US: Deaths from COVID-19 now exceeded 1,000 per day, and nationwide cases surpassed 5.4 million. On August 24, the first documented case of COVID-19 reinfection was confirmed by the University of Hong Kong. Four days afterward, the first documented case of COVID-19 reinfection in the US was confirmed by the Nevada State Public Health Laboratory.

On September 14, 2020, Pfizer BioNTech expanded phase 3 clinical trials of its COVID-19 vaccine to 44,000 participants (the Pfizer/BioNTech vaccine was a 2-shot series given 3 weeks apart and had to be stored at a temperature of -94 degrees Fahrenheit). One week later, Johnson & Johnson began phase 3 clinical trials of its COVID-19 vaccine with 60,000 participants (the J&J vaccine did not need to be frozen and might require just one shot). The next day, it was reported that the death toll in the US from COVID-19 surpassed 200,000. At month's end, the report emerged that the death toll from COVID-19 had reached more than 1 million worldwide in just 10 months.

On October 2, 2020, President Trump tested positive for the SARS CoV-2 virus and was treated at Walter Reed National Military Medical Center. Three days following, more staff at the White House, including the press secretary, tested positive for COVID-19. On October 6, it was announced that food insecurity in the US had reached 52 million people due to the COVID-19 pandemic, which was 17 million more people than pre-pandemic numbers.

On November 4, 2020, one day after the presidential election, the US reported 100,000 new cases of COVID-19 in 24 hours. A week later, the journal *Nature* released a study showing that most COVID-19 cases originated at indoor gathering spaces—places of worship, restaurants, gyms, and grocery stores. Two weeks after large groups gathered for Halloween celebrations, COVID-19 case numbers spiked across the US. On November 16, Moderna's COVID-19 vaccine was found to be 95.4 percent effective in its clinical trial. The next day, Dr. Anthony Fauci discussed the need to understand "long COVID" symptoms like persistent fatigue, shortness of breath, muscle aches, sporadic fevers, and concentration issues, which as many as one-third of patients experienced for weeks or months after contracting COVID-19. On November 18, Pfizer-BioNTech's COVID-19 vaccine was found to be 95 percent effective in their 44,000-person trial. Two days later, and as COVID-19 case numbers in the US surged past 11 million, the Centers for Disease Control and Prevention recommended that Americans stay home for Thanksgiving and avoid contact with all people not living in their household for the last 14 days.

On December 14, 2020, the recorded death toll from COVID-19 in the US surpassed 300,000. That same day, the United Kingdom announced the detection of a new and more contagious COVID-19 variant, B.1.1.7. By December 24, 2020, more than 1 million COVID-19 vaccine doses had been administered in the US in just 10 days, with healthcare workers and older adults living in long-term care facilities being the first to be vaccinated. Two days after Christmas, the Trump administration signed the second COVID Relief Act into law. The bill included 900 billion dollars in funding for enhanced unemployment benefits, business loans, the purchase and distribution of COVID-19 vaccines and testing kits, and direct cash payments of 600 dollars. On December 29, 2020, the first case of the COVID-19 B.1.1.7/"Alpha" variant was detected in the US by the Colorado Department of Health. On the last day of the year—the one-year anniversary of the first reported case of COVID-19 to the World Health Organization—2.8 million people in the US had received a COVID-19 vaccine dose, far short of the nation's goal of 20 million.

On January 18, 2021, the reported death toll from COVID-19 in the US surpassed 400,000. Three days later, the Biden administration reversed the Trump administration's attempt to withdraw from the WHO. Less than a week later, the "Alpha" variant was detected in more than 30 countries and in 12 US states. And on January 25, the first case of the COVID-19 P.1/"Gamma" variant, first identified by scientists in Brazil, was detected in Minnesota. The next day, the number of recorded COVID-19 cases worldwide surpassed 100 million. Two days following this, the first case of the COVID-19 B 1.351/"Beta" variant, first identified by scientists in South Africa, was detected in South Carolina.

On February 21, 2021, the recorded COVID-19 death toll in the US surpassed 500,000.

On March 8, 2021, the Centers for Disease Control and Prevention recommended that people who were fully vaccinated against COVID-19 could safely gather with other fully vaccinated people indoors without masks and without socially distancing. Three days later, it was the first anniversary of the World Health Organization declaring COVID-19 a global pandemic. On March 13, it was announced that more than 100 million COVID-19 vaccine doses had been administered in the US.

On April 21, 2021, it was announced that more than 200 million COVID-19 vaccine doses had been administered in the US. One week later, the Centers for Disease Control and Prevention found that the Pfizer-BioNTech and Moderna mRNA COVID-19 vaccines reduced the risk of hospitalization with SARS-CoV-2 in people ages sixty-five years and older by 94 percent.

On May 14, 2021, the Centers for Disease Control and Prevention found that mRNA COVID-19 vaccines Pfizer-BioNTech and Moderna reduced the risk of infection with the SARS-CoV-2 virus by approximately 94 percent.

On June 1, 2021, the COVID-19 B.1.617.2/"Delta" variant, first identified in India, became the dominant variant in the US. The variant began a third wave of infections during the summer of 2021. Less than a week later, the Centers for Disease Control and Prevention found that the Pfizer-BioNTech and Moderna mRNA COVID-19 vaccines reduced the risk of infection with the SARS-CoV-2 virus by 91 percent and protected against severe illness and hospitalization if a breakthrough infection occurred.

On August 6, 2021, the Centers for Disease Control and Prevention released data which showed that unvaccinated individuals were more than twice as likely to be reinfected with COVID-19 than those who were fully vaccinated after initially contracting the virus (in other words, COVID-19 vaccines offered stronger protection than natural immunity alone).

On September 24, 2021, the Advisory Committee on Immunization Practices (ACIP) recommended Pfizer-BioNTech's COVID-19 vaccine boosters for all people ages sixty-five and older, residents of long-term care settings, people ages fifty to sixty-four with underlying medical conditions, and people ages eighteen to forty-nine with underlying medical conditions and/or who live or work in high-risk settings, to be given at least six months after their primary vaccination series.

On October 6, 2021, the World Health Organization published a clinical case definition of "post COVID-19 condition" or "long COVID." The symptoms of long COVID include, but are not limited to, fatigue, shortness of breath, and/or cognitive dysfunction that persists for at least two months and impacts everyday life, three months from the onset of an initial COVID-19 infection. Three weeks later, the Centers for Disease Control and Prevention released data showing that unvaccinated individuals who had been recently infected with COVID-19 were about five times more likely to be reinfected with the SARS-CoV-2 virus than fully vaccinated individuals with no prior COVID-19 infections.

On November 3, 2021, on the sixth annual One Health Day (a global campaign that highlights the interconnected relationship between people, animals, and their environment), the Centers for Disease Control and Prevention released a statement which noted that more than 400 different animals had been found to be infected with COVID-19 and, as a zoonotic virus, SARS-CoV-2 can spread between people and animals.

On December 1, 2021, the first case of the Omicron variant (first identified by scientists in South Africa) was detected in the US by the California and San Francisco Departments of Public Health. Two weeks later, the recorded death toll from COVID-19 surpassed 800,000 in the US. One in every 100 people ages 65 years and older in the US had died. On

December 20, the Centers for Disease Control and Prevention released data estimating that the Omicron variant is 1.6 times more transmissible than the Delta variant. Three days following, it was announced that Paxlovid remained the preferred oral anti-viral treatment for COVID-19 among adults and children 18 years and older who test positive and were at high risk for progression to severe disease.

On New Year's Day 2022, as Delta and Omicron variants spread, New York State recorded its highest number of new COVID-19 cases in a single day since the pandemic began, with 114,082 new, confirmed cases. Two days later, the US reported nearly 1 million new COVID-19 infections—the highest daily total of any country in the world. The number of hospitalized COVID-19 patients had risen nearly 50 percent in just one week. On January 11, the drug Sotrovimab was found to be effective against both the Delta and Omicron variants. Three days following, the daily average of new COVID-19 infections reported in the US spiked from 119,215 to 805,062. On January 20, a study published in the *American Journal of Epidemiology* found that COVID-19 vaccination had no impact on male or female fertility, but that a COVID-19 infection might be associated with a short-term decline in male fertility. Four days later, the Omicron variant now accounted for approximately 99 percent of all current COVID-19 cases in the US. On the last day of the month, it was estimated that, to date, COVID-19 vaccines had saved at least 250,000 lives and prevented more than 1,000,000 hospitalizations.

On February 4, 2022, the death rate from COVID-19 climbed 30 percent in two weeks amid an Omicron surge, with more than 2,600 people dying from COVID-19 each day. The number of recorded deaths in the US due to COVID-19 surpassed 900,000. Three days later, a study was published in *Nature* showing that even a mild case of COVID-19 appeared to increase the risk of heart problems for one year after infection. The study's authors suggested that COVID-19 might be as much of a risk factor for heart disease as high blood pressure, diabetes, or smoking. On February 11, the Centers for Disease Control and Prevention released data showing that the Omicron variant rose from 1 percent of all infections in the US to 99 percent of all infections in just 6 weeks (compared to 18 weeks for Delta).

On March 2, 2022, the World Health Organization released data showing that the COVID-19 pandemic triggered a 25 percent increase in anxiety and depression worldwide, with young people and women at the highest risk. Three days later, it was reported by the World Health Organization that

10,704,043,684 COVID-19 vaccine doses had been administered worldwide. About 56 percent of the world was now fully vaccinated, but many regions still lacked access, especially on the African continent where less than 20 percent of the total population was currently vaccinated. A week later, the number of recorded deaths due to COVID-19 surpassed 6 million worldwide, with the World Health Organization reporting 6,019,085 confirmed deaths. The number of recorded COVID-19 cases surpassed 450 million worldwide, with the World Health Organization reporting 450,229,635 confirmed infections. March 11 marked the two-year anniversary of the World Health Organization declaring COVID-19 a global pandemic. The next day, the Centers for Disease Control and Prevention estimated that 23 percent of all current COVID-19 infections in the US were caused by the Omicron BA.2 subvariant, with initial data suggesting that BA.2 appeared to be more transmissible than the Omicron BA.1 variant. Less than a week later, the Centers for Disease Control and Prevention released data which showed that adults who received 3 doses of a COVID-19 mRNA vaccine were 94 percent less likely to be put on a ventilator or die from COVID-19 during the Omicron surge, compared to non-vaccinated adults in the US, and that Black adults were currently 4 times more likely to be hospitalized than white adults. On March 24, data from the Census Bureau showed that deaths in the US between 2019 to 2020 increased by approximately 19 percent after the onset of the COVID-19 pandemic in March, 2020. That represented the largest spike in mortality in the US in 100 years. On March 30, the number of recorded deaths due to COVID-19 reached 976,229, with more than 79,853,683 total reported cases of the virus in the US.

On April 13, 2022, it was reported that the Omicron subvariant BA.2 now made up more than 85 percent of all new COVID-19 infections in the US. Nine days later, it was announced that, for the second year in a row, COVID-19 was the third leading cause of death in the US (after heart disease and cancer). On the last day of the month, figures were announced that the current proportion of the US population fully vaccinated against COVID-19 broken down by age group was: 5–11, 28 percent; 12–17, 59 percent; 18–49, 69 percent; 50–64, 80 percent; and 65 years and older, 90 percent.

On May 12, 2022, the number of recorded deaths due to COVID-19 in the US reached 1,000,000. Four days later, researchers from Brown University School of Public Health, Brigham and Women's Hospital, and Harvard T.H. Chan School of Public Health estimated that approximately 50 percent of COVID-19 deaths in the US were vaccine-preventable deaths. On May 28, the weekly average of new COVID-19 infections in the US was now six times higher than it was in 2021. At that time in that month, there were 119,725 new cases reported each week.

On June 1, 2022, the US recorded overall a total of 84,145,569 COVID-19 infections and 1,003,571 deaths from COVID-19. On July 6, 2022, the Centers for Disease Control and Prevention data showed that Omicron subvariants BA.4 and BA.5 were now dominant in the US, making up over 70 percent of new COVID-19 infections.

Since July 2022 and as of May 1, 2023, there were a total number of 6,860,000 deaths from COVID-19 worldwide, and a total of 1,160,000 deaths from COVID-19 in the US.

On May 11, 2023, COVID-19 case and death data reported was discontinued with the end of the public health emergency (PHE) declared by the World Health Organization.

On July 19, 2023, the Centers for Disease Control and Prevention indicated that the coronavirus situation was shifting from the pandemic phase of COVID-19 to the endemic chapter—infection rates were not growing exponentially, and health care systems were not being overwhelmed. The dominant Omicron variant in the US was XBB.1.16 (14.8 percent of cases), followed by XBB.1.9.1 (with 13.2 percent), and XBB.2.3 (with 13 percent). The original Omicron variant was gone, with the listed subvariants replacing it. As of this date, there were currently 26 major variants, most related to the Omicron variant (which was not as serious but was more highly transmissible).

On August 9, 2023, the Centers for Disease Control and Prevention reported that 152,508,460 vaccine doses had been distributed. During the week of August 13–19, there were 15,607 hospitalizations in the US due to COVID-19, and there were 19,357 COVID-related deaths in the US.[26]

As suggested by the article "For Christian Believers, What Does This Pandemic Mean?"[27] there are, and have been, at least three basic and widespread theological responses to COVID-19: First, the virus was interpreted as a punishment from God for the sins humans committed. These sins could range across a wide spectrum from adultery to greed to murder to abortion to the church becoming anemic and not requiring more of its

---

26. Statista, "Coronavirus (COVID-19) Disease Pandemic" (2023); Mathieu et al., "COVID-19 Pandemic."

27. Austriaco, "For Christian Believers."

members to homosexuality to drunkenness to pride to indifference to the poor and oppressed, the marginalized and the vulnerable, to disbelief in God, etc. This is not necessarily the most widespread "answer" for why COVID-19 occurred (among both faith communities and secular society), but it is still very strongly prevalent. According to this point of view, the response of the faithful needs to be repentance and an appeal to God's mercy—through acts of penitence and contrition (i.e., ceasing to do sinful things or failing not to speak up and out about sinful things that others are doing or the society is doing or increasing the number of prayer services and worship occasions, etc.).

From this perspective, God "caused" COVID-19 either through direct means—God singlehandedly intervened in history and nature—or through indirect means—God used nature as an agent (the way God had enlisted nature to punish Sodom and Gomorrah through sulfur and fire [Gen 19:24–25]) and the way God had used a historical figure such as Cyrus II as God's "anointed one" ("Cyrus the *Messiah*" in Isa 45:1) to conquer Babylon and then to liberate the Jews from captivity there.

Of course, the Bible maintains that God not only initially created the world but also continues to be active in it. This activity sometimes involves judgment for unrighteousness. "God's ongoing engagement in the affairs of human life [shows God's] willingness to use extreme measures to accomplish God's purposes."[28] As the apostle Paul proclaims, "the wrath of God is being revealed against all ungodliness and unrighteousness" (Rom 1:18).

Secondly, COVID-19 could be seen as God attempting to draw persons closer to God. It is a wake-up call. "What must God do to get our attention?"[29] The need to repent is always pressing, but especially urgent when it is not known whether one may contract COVID or not, and if contracted, whether that person will die from it. Therefore, one needs to be "prepared to meet one's Maker": "This pandemic provides a reminder that we must repent from our sinfulness while we have time to do so."[30] For, though we may "never know why God allowed some people to get this disease and not others . . . what we do know is that you and I will die and come face-to-face with our Lord to be judged" (2 Cor 5:10).[31]

---

28. Mangrum, "Pandemic as God's Judgment," para. 1.
29. Mangrum, "Pandemic as God's Judgment," para. 7.
30. Horn, "Is COVID-19 a Punishment," para. 10.
31. Horn, "Is COVID-19 a Punishment," para. 12.

"Plagues historically have prompted people to prepare for the afterlife."[32] Thus, in the theological "long run," and in retrospect, COVID-19 will be seen to have been a "blessing."[33]

Thirdly, in the meantime, COVID-19 may present a "test of faith." Will people remain devoted to the God of history and tradition or not? If not, then those persons were not faithful in the first place. If so, then those persons will be rewarded for their loyalty. Their faith will have been galvanized through their experience and strengthened through their suffering. And they will have demonstrated to God that they are legitimate members of the household of believers. Whether we know or not why God chastises God's people with COVID-19, we must remain devoted— for every cross we bear is a test. We are called to "love more," especially to love God more, to love our neighbor more, even in the midst of stress and anxiety, even despite death and difficulty.[34] So, passing this test builds character, and it underscores the hope, the promise, that God will bring good out of this dangerous situation.

Central to these three theological responses to COVID-19 is the underlying assertion and assumption that God is in complete and ultimate control, that nothing happens but by God's direction or by God's permission. Whether it involves punishment, a lesson to be learned, an awareness to be obtained, a blessing to be eventually received, or a test to pass—regardless, God is operating through "meticulous providence," a total governance of all things that occur.

However, theologian Thomas Jay Oord provides a fourth response: From his perspective, COVID-19 does not point to God's anger as a punishment for sin. Nor is COVID-19 something God allowed, as if God could have prevented it, in order to accomplish a higher or good or moral end, such as drawing persons closer to God or demonstrating to humans how much we need God, and as such, constituting an eventual "blessing."

---

32. Mangrum, "Pandemic as God's Judgment."

33. Austriaco, "For Christian Believers," 1.

34. Austriaco, "For Christian Believers," 1; the notion of "test" is very important, on this point, also to Muslims. Omar Ricci, of the Islamic Center of Southern California and national chairman of the Muslim Public Affairs Council (and also a police officer in Los Angeles), entitled one of his *khutbahs*, or sermons, "Thank God for the Coronavirus." In his remarks, he asserted that God should be thanked for reminding us that we are not in control and instead must always be dependent on God. Part of "the test" of COVID-19 is "how Muslims react in difficult times." Coronavirus is not only a test of faith, but also a "solidifying agent of faith" (Qur'an 67:2) (Schnell, "Is the Coronavirus?").

COVID-19 is not a test of faith, according to Oord, in which the greater the horror the stronger faith can become.

Instead, according to Dr. Oord, a God of love would not "will" COVID-19. God is not "smiting" us. In fact, he holds that the coronavirus is not God's will at all. It is also not something that God "permitted" to occur. Instead, it is something that God could not "simply [or singlehandedly] prevent." God is powerful, but God does not control all events; rather, God through God's love is inspiring and persuading creatures and creation, not acting as a Cosmic Dictator. "God never wants, doesn't permit, and can't prevent, evil."[35]

This alternative vision of God's will, God's power, and God's love seems to jibe more relevantly and more reasonably with the human experience of COVID-19. It does not sacrifice divine love on the altar of divine power. It does not appeal to inscrutable mystery as the "reason" why God did not, and does not, intervene when God has the power to do so. However, it stands sharply at odds with the prevalent concept of a God who is omnipotent (God has unlimited power) and the predominant understanding in the Christian tradition of how God works in the world—i.e., God has the power to completely control all things, whether God chooses to do so or not, thus leaving God squarely responsible for the introduction of COVID-19 and the suffering and death that the coronavirus has produced since its inception.

---

35. Oord quoted in Schnell, "Is the Coronavirus?"; Oord, *God Can't*, 181; see Dr. Oord's other excellent and challenging books, *Death of Omnipotence*, esp. 32–40; *God Can't*, ch. 1 and 180–85; and *Uncontrolling Love of God*, ch. 2.

Chapter Four

Plague, Holocaust, Tsunami, and Evolution

THE PLAGUE BY ALBERT Camus was reputed to be the most widely read book during the COVID pandemic when it began in 2020. *The Plague* was first published in French in 1947 and tells the story of a plague assaulting the French Algerian city of Oran. The narrator, whose point of view carries the story, remains unknown until the start of the last chapter, chapter 5 of part 5.

Camus used as source material the cholera epidemic that killed a large proportion of Oran's population in 1849, but he situated the novel in the 1940s. Historically, Oran and its surroundings were struck by disease several times before Camus published his novel: Oran was decimated by the bubonic plague in 1556 and 1678, but all later outbreaks were very far from the scale of the epidemic described in the novel.[1]

In the novel, two key characters stand in opposition to each other—Doctor Bernard Rieux and Father Paneloux. Bernard Rieux is a physician attending patients of the cholera plague in Oran, a city of about 200,000 inhabitants. Rieux treats the first victim of plague and urges the authorities to take action to stop the spread of the epidemic, even though, at first, along with everyone else, the danger seems somewhat unreal. Within a

---

1. Camus, *Plague*, 95; Bertherat et al., "Plague Reappearance," 1459–62.

short while, however, he grasps what is at stake and warns the authorities that unless steps are taken immediately, the epidemic could kill off half the town's population within a couple of months. An atheist, Rieux combats the plague because he is a medical professional and does not do it for any overarching, religious purpose.

Father Paneloux is a devout, educated, and highly respected Jesuit priest. He is well known in the town for having given a series of lectures in which he proclaimed a strong affirmation of Christian belief and admonished the congregation for their religious anemia and moral laxity. Then, during the first stage of the outbreak of the plague, Paneloux preached a sermon in which he insisted that the plague was a scourge sent by God upon those who had hardened their hearts against God and backslid from the Christian faith. As a result, the plague would not strike the innocent, but only those who had been unfaithful and sinful. At the same time, Paneloux also claimed that God was present to offer comfort and hope to the afflicted.

But then Paneloux attended the bedside of the stricken son of a man named Othon and prayed that the boy might be spared. However, the boy died, and after his death, Paneloux told Rieux that although the death of an innocent child in a world ruled by a loving God cannot be rationally explained, it should nonetheless be accepted. However, this was a contradiction of his former assertion that the plague only came to those guilty of sin. Naturally, Paneloux absorbed the inconsistency by appealing to mystery—mere humans could not comprehend that contradiction through the power of reason, so one had to simply cling to one's religious faith.

Subsequently, Paneloux preached another sermon saying that the death of the innocent child was a test of faith. Since God willed the child's death, Christians ought to will it, too. The question of what "kind" of God would will the death of a child was not asked. The child's death was simply accepted as God's will, since God was in total control of whatever happened in the world. So, such a death should be understood in this way.

A few days after preaching this sermon, Paneloux was taken ill. He refused to call for a doctor, trusting in God alone, and died. Since his symptoms did not seem to resemble those of the plague, Dr. Rieux recorded his death as a "doubtful case."

In the prologue of his insightful and suggestive book *God: A New Biography*, written two years before the onslaught of the COVID pandemic, Philip Almond notes that

PLAGUE, HOLOCAUST, TSUNAMI, AND EVOLUTION

> The dispute between Father Paneloux and Doctor Rieux is about a question of fact: Does God exist or not? But it is much more than that. For Rieux, it is not simply a question about what is or is not case. It is also a question about *what kind of God* it is that allows such suffering in the world and yet remains so apparently unconcerned about it.[2]

Echoing Exod 32:35—"God sent a plague on the people, because they made a calf, the one that Aaron made"—Father Paneloux interpreted the plague as punishment delivered by God on the wicked people of the town. "The just have no need to fear," he preached. The "plague is the flail of God and the world His threshing-floor, and implacably He will thresh out His harvest until the wheat is separated from the chaff."[3]

By contrast, Dr. Rieux could not accept a God who stood by while innocent children died in agony. Indeed, if God controls everything that happens—so that disaster is seen as divine punishment—then the peoples' sins must have been unredeemably heinous. Or, alternately, God, for God's own inscrutable reasons, *could* have come to the peoples' aid, but elected not to do so, no matter how widespread the suffering and how deep the agony.

As noted in a previous chapter, *The Canterbury Tales* was begun by Geoffrey Chaucer in the 1380s but remained unfinished. In the "Tale of the Pardoner," three young men who recognize the extent of death caused by the plague set out to kill death in order to eliminate it. They discover a pile of gold, send one companion away, and in his absence plot his demise so that the booty can be divided between two and not three. The absent one plans to poison the others upon his return. So, when he returns, the two kill him but then unknowingly drink the poison he has brought. So, all three are killed, and it is their "sin" that has done them in. The point is that sin is the cause of death. Analogically, the plague is the means of death, and death is the punishment for sin. The bubonic plague is God's penalty for human wrongdoing.

In Chaucer's fourteenth century, the plague was understood to be an instrument of punishment administered by God to mete out justice to sinful people. Again, the assumption was that, since God controls everything that happens, and the plague occurs, then God must be in control of it. And why would God send the plague? Since good things happen to good people,

---

2. Almond, *God*, 5; emphasis mine.
3. Camus, *Plague*, 94.

and bad things happen to bad people, God must have sent the plague because bad people deserved it.

The biblical notion of "covenant theology" and the "Deuteronomistic history" are the foundation for this: What happens in a world governed by God is interpreted to be either a reward for virtuous behavior or a punishment for sinful behavior.

Hebrew Bible and Christian Old Testament scholar Bernhard W. Anderson described the relationship between God and the people in biblical faith as a "covenant" (*berîth*). This covenant was not a binding agreement between equals (a "parity" covenant) but between unequals (a "suzerainty" covenant). It is God who "cuts" (the verb associated with "covenant" [*berîth*]) the covenant, and obligations are placed on both parties in the relationship: The people are to obey God's commandments (*mitzvot*), and God will then "bless" the people. If the people disobey those commands, then God will "curse" them. Anderson puts it this way:

> The suzerainty covenant . . . is more unilateral, for [in the political arena] it is made between a suzerain, a great king, and his vassal, the head of a subordinate state. To his vassal, the suzerain "gives" a covenant, and within the covenant the vassal finds protection and security. As the subordinate party, the vassal is under obligation to obey the commands issued by the suzerain, for the suzerain's words are spoken with the majesty and authority of the covenant author . . . . Blessings will result from obedience to the [covenant] treaty, but curses will fall upon the vassal if he is unfaithful. The king offers protection within the terms of the treaty, but the threat of judgment, even total destruction, falls upon a vassal-state that violates the treaty.[4]

This, in turn, is the filter through which individuals should interpret what happens in their lives in the world. If Israel's forces are defeated on the battlefield, it is because God is punishing them. If they are victorious, it is because God is rewarding them. Even more poignantly, God is with them, "on their side," turning the tide of battle in their favor. "Israel's ups and downs illustrated the basic theological conviction [that] obedience to Yahweh's torah [God's commands] leads to welfare and peace; disobedience results in hardship and defeat."[5]

---

4. Anderson, *Understanding the Old Testament*, 98–100.
5. Anderson, *Understanding the Old Testament*, 184.

PLAGUE, HOLOCAUST, TSUNAMI, AND EVOLUTION

The story of David and Goliath is but one example: Diminutive and outclassed in size, armament, strength, and track record, David is nevertheless victorious because God is on his side and blesses him (and Israel) with victory.

But when Israel loses its sovereignty to Babylon and is defeated by King Nebuchadnezzar in the sixth century BCE and taken into exile, this is interpreted and understood as God's rebuke of Israel for falling away from faithful obedience to God.

Gideon's victory over the Midianites with an inferior force (in fact, Gideon deliberately reduces his numbers, so the text indicates [Judg 7], in order to point to God's providing the victory and not merely the result of Israelite battle prowess) is understood as the result of Israel remaining faithful to God's commandments.

Saul's defeat at the hands of the Philistines is understood as punishment for Saul's having failed to obey God's command (believed to have been given to Saul through the prophet Samuel) to utterly destroy long-term enemies of Israel, the Amalekites, by killing all the men, women, children, and animals (ḥērem). "The word of the Lord came to Samuel: 'I regret that I made Saul king, for he has turned back from following me and has not carried out my commandments'" (1 Sam 15:10). So later, this divine regret resulted in Israel's defeat by the Philistines at Mount Gilboa and Saul's death (1 Sam 31; cf. 1 Chr 10:1–12). "So, Saul died for his unfaithfulness, he was unfaithful to the Lord in that he did not keep the command of the Lord . . . Therefore, the Lord put him to death." (1 Chr 10:13–14).

The Israelites' prevailing over the Canaanites at their stronghold of Megiddo is attributed to the favor of God: Megiddo was the stronghold that commanded the Jezreel Valley, and whoever occupied it could govern trade along the route that ran from Egypt to Mesopotamia.[6] In the last quarter of the twelfth century BCE, the forces of Israel under the leadership of the female judge Deborah defeated the Canaanites under the leadership of Sisera, when a heavy rainstorm caused the Kishon River, which ran through the valley, to overflow. Consequently, the Canaanite chariots got mired in the clay mud (shades of the Egyptian chariots and the crossing of the Red Sea [Sea of Reeds] by the Hebrews in the Exodus!), and the Israelites triumphed.

The Song of Deborah in Judg 5 points to the religious meaning of the victory: The storm points to the active presence of God in both history and

---

6. Anderson, *Understanding the Old Testament*, 196.

nature to reward God's faithful people by giving them the victory. "No array of human forces can stand against *Yahweh* [God], the Divine Warrior, who comes to the aid of Israel in the fury of a thunderstorm."[7]

Indeed, this notion of reward for faithfulness and punishment for unfaithfulness is the premise of prophetic activity in Israel: When Israel, and individual leaders within it, uphold the commands of God, Israel is successful, as are the leaders. When Israel, and leaders within it, turn their backs on the commands of God, the nation is defeated, and its leaders are deposed.

God's power and purpose (will) are unquestioned and preserved, and humans' accountability and responsibility determine their fate. Good things are indicators that they are being blessed; bad things are signals that they are being cursed. Good things come to good people; bad things come to bad people. "*Yahweh* [God] alone controls the events of history and the powers of nature."[8] And God does so on the basis of reward and punishment.

Hebrew Bible and Christian Old Testament scholar Walter Brueggemann chimes in that "in a tightly ordered world, good people prosper, and evil people suffer." This is the "transactional mode of covenant."[9] "The Lord watches over the way of the righteous, but the way of the wicked will perish" (Ps 1:6). This is shorthand for the "two great recitals of blessing and curse in the Torah":[10]

> In spite of these punishments, you have not turned back to me, but continue hostile to me, then I, too, will continue to be hostile to you. I myself will strike you sevenfold for your sins. I will bring the sword against you, executing vengeance for the covenant; and if you withdraw within your cities, I will send pestilence among you, and you shall be delivered into enemy hands. When I break your staff of bread, ten women shall bake your bread in a single oven, and they shall dole out your bread by weight; and though you eat, you shall not be satisfied. (Lev 26:23–26)
>
> The Lord will make the pestilence cling to you until it has consumed you off the land that you are entering to possess. The Lord will afflict you with consumption, fever, inflammation, with fiery heat, and drought, and with blight and mildew . . . . The Lord

---

7. Anderson, *Understanding the Old Testament*, 197.
8. Anderson, *Understanding the Old Testament*, 108.
9. Brueggemann, *Virus as a Summons*, 2.
10. Brueggemann, *Virus as a Summons*, 2.

will cause you to be defeated before your enemies .... A people whom you do not know will eat up the fruit of your ground and of all your labors; you shall be continually abused and crushed, and driven mad by the sight that your eyes shall see. (Deut 28:21–34)

Thus, in the Deuteronomy-covenant tradition, *God* sends pestilence: "I will strike down the inhabitants of this city, both human beings and animals; they shall die of a great pestilence" (Jer 21:6). And most times, the "triad of divine punishment" involves sword, pestilence, famine.

The prophetic tradition reiterates this triad: For example, Jer 21:9 says, "Those who stay in this city [Jerusalem] shall die by the sword, by famine, and by pestilence; but those who go out and surrender to the Chaldeans who are besieging you shall live and shall have their lives as a prize of war." Jeremiah 24:10 states, "I will send sword, famine, and pestilence upon them, until they are utterly destroyed from the land that I gave to them and their ancestors."[11]

Jeremiah 42:17 warns, "All the people who have determined to go to Egypt to settle there shall die by the sword, by famine, and by pestilence; they shall have no remnant or survivor from the disaster that I am bringing upon them."[12] Jeremiah 44:13 continues, "I will punish those who live in the land of Egypt, as I have punished Jerusalem, with the sword, with famine, and with pestilence." Ezekiel 6:11–13a echoes the same theme: "Thus says the Lord God: 'Clap your hands and stamp your foot, and say, Alas for all the vile abominations of the house of Israel! For they shall fall by the sword, by famine, and by pestilence. Those far off shall die of pestilence; those nearby shall fall by the sword, and any who are left and are spared shall die of famine. Thus, I will send my fury upon them. And you shall know that I am the Lord.'" "'The plague' (along with sword and famine) is an instrument of divine punishment against those who violate the covenantal order of creation willed by God."[13]

---

11. See also Jer 29:18; 32:36; 34:17; 38:2.

12. See also Jer 42:22.

13. Brueggemann, *Virus as a Summons*, 4. However, as Brueggemann points out, the sequence of "plagues" in the narrative of the Exodus is different, for here the ten sequential maladies are more a demonstration of God's power than a punishment (although some scholars argue that it is pharaoh who is being punished for his brutality regarding Hebrew slaves in the past and for his recalcitrance in being unwilling to let them go free in the present). "The aim is to exhibit the capacity of the creator God to mobilize the various elements of creation in the service of divine intentionality" (*Virus as a Summons*, 5).

But, of course, good persons are not always rewarded, and bad persons are not always punished. Indeed, it doesn't always work out this way, and good people have terrible tragedies happen to them, and bad people get away with being evil with no negative repercussions. The fact that the "transactional covenant" schematic does not work out is the basic premise of the book of Job. Job is a corrective to the "normal" Hebrew Scripture way of understanding the good and bad things that occur: And that is, good things happen to good people, bad things happen to bad people—covenantal theology. Obey the covenant and be good, and God will bless you; disobey the covenant, and God will punish you.

But Job is a good person who nevertheless suffers! How can this be? His friends—Eliphaz (Job 4, 15, 22), Bildad (Job 8, 18, 25), and Zophar (Job 11, 20)—challenge him to "'fess up" and repent, for surely he has done something to warrant the tragedies that have befallen him. Yet Job insists that he has not committed any immoral behavior for which what happens to him would be justified.

At one point, God challenges Job by asking him, "Where were you when I created the heavens and the earth?" (Job 38:4f; see Job 40:9) and thus putting him in his place. The message here is that Job has no basis upon which to question God: Job is a mere mortal, and what right has he to challenge the Immortal? The ending of the book of Job points to the mystery of God and Job's acknowledgment of God's superiority and human beings' inferiority, of God's sovereign transcendence and men and women's piddly inability to see the cosmic picture and to understand the ways of God (see Isa 55:8–9).

And for Job's persistence in having faith—despite the earthly and theological injustice with which he grapples—and for his repentance (Job 42:6), he is rewarded at the end of the story by having his fortunes doubly restored (42:10–15) and enjoying a long life of 140 years as a reward (42:16–17).

In some thought, Jewish and otherwise, reward and punishment are meted out not only in this world, but also in the world to come. Reward for a person's virtuous behavior may occur in the present world but also in the afterlife. The same is true for punishment for the one who does evil. "This world is the place where one, so to speak, accumulates a credit or a debit balance of good or bad actions, the results of which one enjoys or suffers in the world to come."[14]

---

14. Rabinowitz, "Reward and Punishment."

> God exercises a miraculous and absolutely just providence over humankind. Thus, God has revealed in the Torah the commandments human beings are to keep. Persons are rewarded or punished in accordance with their obedience or disobedience of the Torah. Their deeds are known to God and recorded by God. Reward and punishment are meted out both in this world and the next . . . "reward and punishment" is one of the three fundamental principles of Judaism.[15]

Following the Nazi program of extermination of Jews as their answer to the *Judenfrage* (the Jewish Question), the notion of good things being a divine reward for goodness and bad things being a divine punishment for evil, and the credibility of a God who operates providentially in the world in such a manner, fell under scrutiny and experienced great strain.

> The phrase "after Auschwitz" became a theological code word for the question of whether it is still possible to believe in the election of Israel and the God who acts in history, especially Jewish history, in view of the Holocaust.[16]

For the first two decades following World War II, there was little to no Jewish concern with the Holocaust as a challenging and crucial problem. But then in the late sixties, Rabbi Richard L. Rubenstein made the statement that he could no longer accept the credibility of "the traditional belief in the existence of the biblical God who elects Israel and acts decisively in history, because such a God would have to bear ultimate responsibility for Auschwitz."[17] Rubenstein maintained that there was no divine guidance to this event, nor could any divine purpose be assigned it. He rejected any suggestion that Hitler, Goebbels, Himmler, and Eichmann were in any way the agents of the God of history.

In Rubenstein's view, it is impossible to face honestly the agonizing truth of the Holocaust and continue to believe in an omnipotent and benevolent God:

> Having lived through this ultimate expression of human cruelty and degradation, we can only deny the traditional God. . . . One need not have the obscenity of Auschwitz before one's eyes in order to be moved to deny God. Human suffering of whatever dimensions, so long as it is unjust and unmerited, is sufficient

---

15. Reines, "Medieval Jewish Philosophy."
16. Rubenstein, *After Auschwitz*, 46; see also Rubenstein, *Religious Imagination*.
17. Rubenstein, *After Auschwitz*, 204; see 153.

to raise profound doubts about the existence of the God of our religious tradition.... If God's omnipotence makes Him responsible for human suffering, then we should revile Him and rebel against Him. Such a God is unworthy of man's loyalty.... The real objections against a personal or theistic God come from the irreconcilability of the claim of God's perfection with the hideous human evil tolerated by such a God.... A God who tolerates the suffering of even one innocent child is either infinitely cruel or hopelessly indifferent.[18]

Elie Wiesel's renowned reflections on his experience and survival in the camps gave the problem "a literary immediacy."[19] Although Wiesel would raise hard questions and voice strong criticisms of the absence or silence of God, he maintained the traditional God-concept of his Jewish faith, albeit a Job-like upholding of the unintelligibility of the Holocaust and the mystery of God. He would be joined by the famed Jewish thinker Emil Fackenheim in this upholding of the traditional God-concept, for Fackenheim argued that to reject the traditional God was "to give Hitler the victory."[20]

Wiesel, in his preface to *Night*, confesses that

> I don't know *how* I survived; I was weak, rather shy; I did nothing to save myself. A miracle? Certainly not. If heaven could or would perform a miracle for me, why not for others more deserving than myself? It was nothing more than chance.[21]

Elie Wiesel seems to waver—as a devout student of rabbinic commentary on Torah (the Talmud)—and as an inquirer into Jewish mysticism in cabbalism and its chief text, the *Zohar*: He has a deep faith in the God of Israel who chose the Jewish people to be in a special relationship with him and who delivered them from capture and annihilation at the Red Sea ("Sea of Reeds"—*Yam sûf*) and who provided them with quail and manna in the wilderness and led them into battle and fought alongside the Israelites in their altercations with other peoples in the "land flowing with milk and honey" and with warring neighbors from surrounding countries. He believed that when God was "displeased by Noah's generation, God brought down the Flood. When Sodom lost God's favor, God caused the heavens to

---

18. Rubenstein, *op.cit.*

19. Wiesel, *Night*.

20. Emil Fackenheim, *The Christian Century* 87.18 (May 6, 1970), quoted in LeMoult, "Thou Shalt Not Let Hitler Win."

21. Wiesel, *Night*, vii–viii.

PLAGUE, HOLOCAUST, TSUNAMI, AND EVOLUTION

rain down fire and damnation."[22] But he also cannot reconcile this mighty God, this warrior God, this God who was the "father" of the Jewish people and they were his "children," with the experience of brutality and murder in the concentration camps.

> If God causes all things to occur that occur, then "Why, but why, would I bless God? Every fiber in me rebelled. Because He caused thousands of children to burn in His mass graves? Because He kept six crematoria working day and night, including Sabbath and the Holy Days? Because in His great might, He had created Auschwitz, Birkenau, Buna, and so many other factories of death? How could I say to Him: Blessed be Thou, Almighty, Master of the Universe, who chose us among all nations to be tortured day and night, to watch as our fathers, our mothers, our brothers end up in the furnaces? Praised be Thy Holy Name, for having chosen us to be slaughtered on Thine altar?"[23]

At some points, Wiesel seems to lose faith and echo the words of fellow Holocaust survivor Primo Levi, "There is Auschwitz. And so there cannot be God."[24] Wiesel proclaims:

> Never shall I forget that night, the first night in camp, that turned my life into one long night seven times sealed. Never shall I forget that smoke. Never shall I forget the small faces of the children whose bodies I saw transformed into smoke under a silent sky. Never shall I forget those flames that consumed my faith forever. Never shall I forget the nocturnal silence that deprived me for all eternity of the desires to live. Never shall I forget those moments that murdered my God and my soul and turned my dreams to ashes. Never shall I forget those things, even were I condemned to live as long as God Himself. Never.[25]

In the story of the hanging of the young boy who is too light to have his neck immediately broken by the noose when the chair is tipped over and consequently flails and twitches for over thirty minutes before succumbing, Wiesel seems to suggest from within himself (when he hears the question, "where is God?") that God is hanging on the gallows with the boy, that God

---

22. Wiesel, *Night*, 68.

23. Wiesel, *Night*, 67.

24. Quoted in Click, "Elie Wiesel's Unique Journey," 8. cf. Levi, *Survival in Auschwitz*, 157–58.

25. Wiesel, *Night*, 34.

has been murdered along with him, that the notion of God he has inherited and which he holds is incompatible with what has just happened.

But at other points he seems to shout at the silence of God. Implied here is the affirmation that God exists, and that God has the power to intervene and does not and is therefore silently absent. Wiesel continued to protest this silence of God, the incongruity of silence and inaction with the barbaric horrors of the camps. In an interview with Krista Tippett of National Public Radio, Wiesel explains: "I never doubted God's existence. I have problems with God's apparent silence, you know, the old questions of theology. And they are topical even today."[26]

At a gathering of religious studies students during his annual visit to Chapman College and the small Holocaust memorial room there, Wiesel indicated that he still protests the silence of God, not from outside faith but from the inside. His protest was not a denial of God, but an act of faith. And within the camp on Yom Kippur, when Jews are required to fast from food and drink (unless doing so is an impairment to health), he chose not to fast as "a symbol of rebellion, of protest against Him [God]" for God's silence and inactivity.[27]

In that same interview with Krista Tippett, Elie Wiesel indicated his accusation, his anger, and his protest against God:

> Some people who read my first book, *Night*, they were convinced that I broke with the faith and broke with God. Not at all. I never divorced God. It is because I believed in God that I was angry at God, and still am. The tragedy of the believer, it is deeper than the tragedy of non-believers.

And later, he adds:

> My faith is tested, wounded, but it's here. So, whatever I say, it's always from inside faith, even when I speak the way I occasionally do about the problems I had, questions I had. Within my traditions, you know, it is permitted to question God, even to take Him to task.[28]

---

26 Tippett, "Elie Wiesel." Cf. Elie Wiesel, *The Trial of God*, a play in which Jewish survivors of a sixteenth-century pogrom put God on trial for the terrible things God has allowed to happen to them. "Either God is responsible or He is not. If He is, let's judge Him; if He is not, let Him stop judging us" (from the play, the character Berish speaking).

27. Wiesel, *Night*, 69.

28. Wiesel, "Tragedy of the Believer."

And, at some points, Wiesel asks not whether God exists, but rather what kind of God the God who exists is. And although he sometimes asks, "*Where* is God?" at other times, he asks, "*What* is God?" Is God the God of goodness and love and power, or is God a "cosmic Sadist," to borrow a phrase from C. S. Lewis in *A Grief Observed*? The question for Lewis was not whether God existed, but rather whether God was sadistic. "Not that I am (I think) in much danger of ceasing to believe in God. The real danger is of coming to believe such dreadful things about Him. The conclusion I dread is not 'So, there's no God after all,' but 'So this is what God's really like.'"[29]

At still other points, Wiesel acknowledges that the ways of God are mysterious. Wiesel here did not question God's existence, he questions God's justice: "Some of the men spoke of God: His mysterious ways, the sins of the Jewish people, and the redemption to come. As for me, I had ceased to pray. I concurred with Job! I was not denying His existence, but I doubted His absolute justice."[30] In the end, Wiesel does not understand how the horrors and murders can "fit" within the concept and believe in a God who is all-loving, all-powerful, and all-knowing, but he clings to that concept and belief regardless.

In fact, when Wiesel is liberated from Auschwitz in April of 1945, he joins with a group of other adolescents in order to celebrate their freedom by praying the *Kaddish*, the Jewish prayer for the dead.[31] And, when Wiesel returns to Auschwitz for the first time, the only words he can utter inside the camp are the words of the *Kaddish*, plus a reading from his book where he laments that he will never be able to forget the smoke of the crematoria. The *Kaddish* prayer, a prayer offered by mourners after the death of a loved one, does not talk about death or the deceased. Instead, it addresses, salutes, the majesty and sovereignty of God:

> Magnified and sanctified is the great name of God throughout the world, which was created according to Divine will. May the rule of peace be established speedily in our time, unto us, and unto the entire household of Israel. And let us say: Amen.

---

29. Lewis, *Grief Observed*, 16–17. Later in the book, Lewis affirms and laments that his late wife, Joy, is "in God's hands. But if so, she was in God's hands all the time, and I have seen what they did to her here" (27).

30. Wiesel, *Night*, 45.

31. Weintrob, "Honoring Elie and Marion Wiesel."

Inscrutable and enigmatic, God's ways are not our ways (Isa 55:8–9). As Wiesel puts it, "Man is too insignificant, too limited, to even try to comprehend God's mysterious ways."[32]

Anne Frank, the daughter of Amsterdam factory owner Otto Frank, emigrated with her family from Germany to Holland when she was four years old. When her sister, Margo, was summoned by the German occupation forces after the defeat and occupation of Holland, the family knew they had to go into hiding. A secret annex in the upstairs of the factory (the *achterhuis*) served as the dwelling place of Anne, her father and mother, her sister, and four others who appealed to the Franks for help. They successfully hid in the attic for 761 days from July 6, 1942, until August 4, 1944, when they were apprehended by the authorities.

During that time, Anne kept a diary,[33] a gift that had been given to her on her thirteenth birthday on June 12, 1942. The diary has been translated into more than seventy languages and has sold over thirty million copies. For many persons, it is their first, and unfortunately only, exposure to the history of the Holocaust.

Anne had a traditional concept of God—she believed that God could do anything God wanted to. Her best friend and neighbor in Amsterdam, Hanneli (Hannah Pick-Goslar), was taken away to the concentration camps, and Anne was powerless to help: "I can only stand by and watch while other people suffer and die. All I can do is pray to God to bring her back to us."[34]

Anne also questions why Hanneli is destined for death (ironically Hanneli survives the camps, moves to Jerusalem and becomes a nurse, and dies at the age of ninety-three on October 28, 2022), while Anne is alive and in hiding. "Why have I been chosen to live, while she's probably going to die?"[35] Here Anne affirms the traditional view that everything that happens is God's will, and life and death are meted out according to divine purpose and celestial plan. Of course, ultimately and tragically, Anne is *not* going to live, and after her arrest, will die of typhus in April of 1945 in Bergen-Belsen concentration camp. This traditional view would also affirm that Anne's death was divinely ordained.

---

32. Wiesel, *Night*, 76.
33. Frank, *Diary of a Young Girl*.
34. Frank, *Diary of a Young Girl*, 161.
35. Frank, *Diary of a Young Girl*, 162.

Still concerned about Hanneli, Anne will later pray, "Dear God, watch over her and bring her back to us."[36] And later, "The most you can do is pray for God to perform a miracle and save at least some of them."[37] The assumption remains, first, that God is in control and, second, that perhaps Anne's beseeching God to act in Hanneli's behalf will be successful.

In a subsequent diary entry—January 30, 1944—Anne is by herself in the dark at the top of the stairs, and she watches the German planes flying back and forth. She calms herself by looking up "at the sky and trusting in God." God will protect her and her family, *if* that is God's will.[38]

Later that year after a break-in, she interprets their not being detected as an indication of God's protection: "None of us have [sic] ever been in such danger as we were that night. God was truly watching over us."[39] But when they were arrested in August 1944, was God *not* watching over them? It seems that one cannot have it both ways.

Anne believed that the suffering of the Jewish people had a purpose, a divine reason for occurring: "It's God who has made us the way we are [as Jews], but it's also God who will lift us up again . . . . The reason, the only reason, we have to suffer is so that our religion will teach the world about goodness."[40] That is, some good result, divinely intentioned or purposed, will come from horrible suffering, also divinely caused or permitted.

She continues this theme in her writing: "God has never deserted our people. Through the ages Jews have had to suffer, but through the ages they've gone on living, and the centuries of suffering have only made them stronger."[41] This "suffering will galvanize you" perspective, though sometimes true—humans *can* become stronger through the hard and harsh experiences they have—does not seem to apply when Anne and so many other Jews were brutally murdered. How is a lasting galvanization a positive result when one is dead?

One of the other persons hiding in the attic, Mr. Voskuijl, has cancer, and it is a hopeless case. Anne therefore appeals to divine assistance since "only God can help him now."[42] The underlying perspective and hope here

---

36. Frank, *Diary of a Young Girl*, 169.
37. Frank, *Diary of a Young Girl*, 169.
38. Frank, *Diary of a Young Girl*, 194.
39. Frank, *Diary of a Young Girl*, 281.
40. Frank, *Diary of a Young Girl*, 282.
41. Frank, *Diary of a Young Girl*, 283.
42. Frank, *Diary of a Young Girl*, 294.

are that God is intimately engaged with the world and is capable of intervening to arrest and reverse Mr. Voskuijl's medical condition. This notion of miraculous divine intervention would also apply to the Holocaust—the assumption is that God *can* do it *if* God so chooses.

In a prayer on the radio following government-in-exile Dutch Queen Wilhemina's address to her citizens, God was asked "to take care of the Jews, all those in concentration camps and prisons and everyone working in Germany."[43] This once again assumes that God *can* take care of the Jews. Since God did *not* take care of all of them—and chance and happenstance seemed to determine life and death—did God *choose* not to take care of them, even though God *could* have done so? Did God choose not to do so because God wanted to preserve the human freedom of the Nazis and to do so would be to abrogate the genuineness of their human choice to do good or to do evil? Or was God not able to do this because God's power is not unlimited and God, in effect, cannot do everything God would prefer to do?

After an unsuccessful assassination attempt on Hitler, it was broadcast that "the Führer owes his life to 'Divine Providence.'" Anne goes on to conclude that "perhaps Providence is deliberately biding its time getting rid of Hitler."[44] Again, the assumption is that God is in control of everything that occurs. But if divine providence is truly in charge, then why did God *not* take out Hitler using *Wehrmacht* (German Army) resisters like Colonel Claus von Stauffenberg, one of the leaders of the assassination plot to rid Germany of Hitler? Or, more directly, why did God not strike Hitler dead with a lightning bolt for his heinous crimes, the way that God sent fire and brimstone/sulfur from heaven as a natural disaster to destroy Sodom and Gomorrah (Gen 19:24–25; Luke 17:28–30) for their sins?

It should be noted that Hitler himself believed that his narrow escape from the bomb blast from the briefcase left by Colonel von Stauffenberg in the Führer's Wolf's Lair field headquarters was an act of divine providence, or at least his followers did. He and they concluded that Hitler's miraculous absconding was a reaffirmation of his role as Germany's messiah or savior who would restore greatness to the nation. Hitler became convinced that fate had spared him when the assassination attempt known as "Operation Valkyrie" failed:

> I regard this as a confirmation of the task imposed upon me by Providence—and that nothing is going to happen to me.... [T]he

---

43. Frank, *Diary of a Young Girl*, 316.
44. Frank, *Diary of a Young Girl*, 359.

great cause which I serve will be brought through its present perils and . . . everything can be brought to a good end.[45]

In other words, Hitler and his henchmen believed that God had sanctioned the Führer's rule and goals and methods.

From Anne's *Diary* and from the common theological understanding, the traditional concept of God involves a deity who controls all things, who can be sought for protection, and who will ultimately bring good things out of terrible situations.

American Rabbi Harold Kushner also addresses the situation of God and suffering, and of the biblical figure Job and justice, in light of covenantal theology and the "transactional mode of relationship" between God and the people. In his book *When Bad Things Happen to Good People*, written over four decades ago, he responds to the death of his fourteen-year-old son, Aaron, who died in 1977 of the disease Hutchinson-Gilford Progeria Syndrome, a malady so rare that only one in twenty million gets it, a genetic mutation that occurs randomly and not genetically from parents, and a progressive disorder that causes children to age very rapidly. At any given time, there are only four hundred children in the world living with Progeria.[46]

In this book, Rabbi Kushner reveals that the typical, traditional answers for how a good, loving, and powerful God and Aaron's condition could simultaneously exist were simply not satisfactory. So, he argues for a concept of God that preserves divine benevolence, but not omnipotence: God is good, but God is not all-powerful and cannot prevent evil, pain, and suffering.

In addition, Kushner examines the figure of Job in his book *The Book of Job: When Bad Things Happened to a Good Person*.[47] In that book, he argues that three assertions may be made when tragedy occurs to the figure Job: Job is a good man; God is all-good; God is all-powerful. He goes on to conclude that you can have any two of these as true, but not all three: If Job is a good man, and if God is all-powerful, then God must not be good and just, because Job is being wrongly punished; he is an innocent man. If God is all-good, and God is all-powerful, then Job must not be a good man, because he must deserve what he gets as punishment and justice. If Job is a good man and God is all-good, then God must not be all-powerful because

---

45. Steinweis, "Idea of Eliminating the Leadership"; cf. Schramm, "Anatomy of a Dictator," 88–91.

46. Kushner, *When Bad Things Happen*.

47. Kushner, *Book of Job*.

what happens to Job does not come from God, and God is not powerful enough to prevent it from occurring.

Again, Kushner's conclusions are that God is good and that God is not unlimited in God's power; thus, Kushner opts for the third model. Therefore, God cannot control human behavior because for God to require humans to act justly would only be a form of coercion. Regarding the tsunami that killed a quarter of a million people and an earthquake that ravaged Haiti, Kushner said, "God is moral; nature is not."[48] God does not arbitrarily interfere with laws of nature.

If God were either all-powerful, but not kind, or thoroughly kind and loving, but not totally powerful, Kushner would rather compromise God's power and affirm God's love.

Tsunamis are categorized as a "natural evil."[49] One catastrophic tsunami was that which struck off Sumatra, an Indonesian island, on December 26, 2004, at 7:59 a.m. local time. It registered a magnitude of 9.1 and within one half-hour had produced waves more than 100 feet high, killing 170,000 people and laying waste buildings and highways. Within an hour afterward, beaches in southern Thailand were hit by the tsunami, killing 5,400, including 2,000 foreign tourists. In Sri Lanka, UNICEF officials estimated that 30,000 people were killed, at least 10,000 of whom were children.[50]

In all, 225,000 people were killed across 12 countries. David Bentley Hart, in his book *The Doors of the Sea: Where Was God in the Tsunami?* reports that commentators saw this horror in Asia as proof either of God's power or of God's non-existence. "How could a good and loving God—if such exists—allow such suffering?"[51] Or cause it in the first place?

Hart feels compelled to speak out about this tragedy not so much because of those who doubted God's existence, but because of those who offered inappropriate, unsatisfactory, and vapid "answers."

> I still find myself less perturbed by the sanctimonious condescension of many of those who do not believe, than by either the

---

48. Kushner, *Book of Job*, 197. See also Caplan, "Q and A"; and Kaifes, "'Book of Job.'"

49. Philosophers typically divide evil into two categories—moral evil and natural evil. Moral evil is the result of the abuse of human freedom by persons who choose to do evil. Natural evil is the result of the forces of nature; humans do not necessarily "cause" natural evil, but are the recipients of it through natural rhythms, cycles, and "laws."

50. Information Architects of *Encyclopaedia Britannica*, "Indian Ocean Tsunami of 2004"; Editors of *Encyclopedia Britannica*, "Sunda Strait."

51. Hart, *Doors of the Sea*.

gelid dispassion or the shapeless sentimentality of certainty of those who do.[52]

The book is composed of two chapters—"Universal Harmony" and "Divine Victory"—with each comprising five brief sections. "Universal Harmony" surveys the variety of responses to the tsunami event, and "Divine Victory" points to Hart's conviction that

> God is utterly good and goodness itself. His work in Christ is a work of judgment and victory, and his eschatological revelation will be the same. God will not bring every event in history into "one great synthesis but will judge much of history false and damnable ... and will strike off the fetters in which creation languishes."[53]

Hart's own theological response is not to see the tsunami as the providential will of God, but rather to understand it as God's struggle between the "rebellious powers that enslave the world and the God who loves it wholly." That is, God is not the "immediate cause of all evil in the world" nor is the tsunami any sort of "final balancing of accounts," removing evil from the "level of offense" and "thereby making it meaningful." God does not make this suffering "worth it" in the end, "as though divine ends justify the most horrific means."[54] The entirety of history is not the predication of a predetermined divine will. He believes that if it were, that would provide "an excellent moral case for atheism."[55]

There is, of course, some comfort to be derived from the thought that everything that occurs at the level of secondary causality—in nature or history—is governed not only by a transcendent providence but by a universal teleology (purpose) that makes every instance of pain and loss an indispensable moment in a grand scheme whose ultimate synthesis will justify all things. But one should consider the price at which that comfort is purchased: It requires us to believe in and love a God whose good ends will be realized not only in spite of—but entirely by way of—every cruelty, every fortuitous misery, every catastrophe, every betrayal, every sin the world has ever known; it requires us to believe in the eternal spiritual necessity of a child dying an agonizing death from diphtheria, of a young mother ravaged by cancer, of tens of thousands of Asians swallowed in an instant by the sea,

---

52. Hart, *Doors of the Sea*, 92.
53. Hart, *Doors of the Sea*, 104.
54. Hart, *Doors of the Sea*, 92–93, 25–29.
55. Hart, *Doors of the Sea*, 30.

of millions murdered in death camps and gulags and forced famines (and so on). It is a strange thing indeed to seek peace in a universe rendered morally intelligible at the cost of a God rendered morally loathsome.[56]

Because God's love and goodness are so encompassing, God cannot cause evil and suffering, or even use them in the service of God's will. As a result, divine providence is not divine causation, and therefore, a tsunami has no place in the mysterious, overarching purposes of God. However, for Hart, God may permit what God does not will, so that "the integrity of the world and its limited sphere of freedom might be maintained. This lies beyond our full comprehension, for the mystery of God and of God's ways is unfathomable."[57]

Philosophy professor Bailie Peterson has noted that, in Western Christian thought, God is traditionally described as a being that possesses at least three necessary properties—omniscience (all-knowing), omnipotence (all-powerful), and omnibenevolence (supremely good). "Omnipresence" (all-present; present everywhere) may be a fourth divine characteristic.[58]

The notion of "omnipotence" can be traced all the way back to the premier theologian of the early church and recognized as one of the greatest theologians in Christian history, Augustine of Hippo (354–430 CE). Augustine defined God's omnipotence as meaning that "God can do anything that God wills to do."[59] Therefore, he interpreted everything that occurred as in accord with God's will. Although human free will was preserved in his thought—tracing sin to its beginnings in the Garden of Eden when Adam and Eve were disobedient to God through the temptation of the serpent (which Augustine and early Christian tradition identified as the fallen angel, Satan)—he understands that humans used their choices to turn away from God and "sinned." This fall of humanity required God to send God's Son, Jesus, in order that fallen humanity might be able to be reconciled to God. All suffering, then, was a punishment for sin or a result of sin.

In her insightful doctoral dissertation, Samantha Thompson recognizes this dichotomy:[60] Humans suffer on the one hand because their poor choices result in self-inflicted suffering; but on the other hand, God also causes suffering as divinely inflicted punishment for sins that humans

---

56. Hart, *Doors of the Sea*, 98–99.
57. Hart, *Doors of the Sea*, 90–91.
58. Peterson, "Concept of God."
59. Augustine of Hippo, *City of God*, ch. 10.
60. Thompson, "Augustine on Suffering and Order."

commit. Thompson criticizes the prevalent view that Augustine is completely obsessed with sin, as a pathologist is focused on disease, and that Augustine is more concerned with the disease of sin than the remedy. Her appeal to "order" in the universe is the contextual way she suggests that Augustine holds this dichotomy or contradiction together. God's justice that metes out suffering is both retributive and remedial: It is intended by God to give persons what they justly deserve but also serve as a tool for assisting persons to grow morally and become better persons. The latter helps with one's "soul development."

Augustine realizes that bad things happen to bad people and to good people alike. He tries to explain this by stating that suffering makes no distinction between persons based on their relative virtue. "The everyday gifts of God, as also the disasters of humanity, happen to those with good lives and those with evil lives, without distinction."[61] As a result, "temporal goods and temporary evils . . . befall good and bad alike."[62] "Original sin" is not just an event of disobedience in the Garden, it is also the "condition," the disruption of order, that allows this to be the case. Suffering is caused by the sins of humans, but also by the condition of original sin that plagues and characterizes all humans.

But, in any case, God is ultimately in control. God is omnipotent, and God's will cannot be finally frustrated. What happens is what God intends to happen, and divine punishment for sins and original sin is warranted. The "mystery" of how bad things can happen to good people—as in the figure of Job, for example—is "solved" through the reality of original sin.

The phrase "red in tooth and claw"—i.e., involving savage or merciless conflict or competition—is often attributed to Charles Darwin. But it actually was penned by Alfred Lord Tennyson (1809-92):

> A thousand types are gone:
> I care for nothing, all shall go . . .
> [Nature is a world of strife and conflict and violence]
> Nature red in tooth and claw.[63]

Tennyson, who was poet laureate for over four decades from 1850 until his death, had learned of the brutality of nature not from Darwin's theory of evolution (*Origin of Species* was not published until 1859 after Tennyson's

---

61. Augustine of Hippo, *City of God*, ch. 2.2.
62. Augustine of Hippo, *City of God*, ch. 1.8.
63. Tennyson, *In Memoriam A.H.H.*, canto 56.

In Memoriam), but from geology: "Catastrophism" was learned by Tennyson while a student at Cambridge University, and this theory maintains that the fossil record is the result of short, sudden, and violent disasters that occurred between longer, steady periods of geologic time. Geology has shown that so many earlier species have gone extinct, and this prefigures the Darwinian view of nature. "More than 99 percent of all organisms that have ever lived on Earth are extinct."[64]

Tennyson inevitably asked, Is this humanity's fate, too, to follow the dinosaur and the woolly mammoth to extinction? Other "types" are insensible animals, but it is quite another thing for *Homo sapiens*, he reflected, who are aware of what it is to live and die, and who have tried their best to please and placate God by praying to God and by building churches and temples in God's honor, to be allowed to die off.

Tennyson could personally relate to this "dying off": His young friend Arthur Henry Hallam (1811–33) had died in his prime at age twenty-two in Vienna due to a cerebral hemorrhage. Hallam had fallen in love with Tennyson's sister, Emilia, when she was eighteen, and they became engaged.

Impersonal nature either operating within the sphere of God's activity or self-regulating beyond the arena of God's providence was a pressing, thorny issue at the time. Biblical interpretation was at stake (God was portrayed in sacred literature as active and controlling in history and in nature, the Genesis creation accounts being but one example) and faith seemed at risk (did science and natural law make God superfluous?).

After an unsuccessful year studying medicine at the University of Edinburgh, and at his father's insistence, Charles Darwin (1809–82) went to Cambridge University in 1828 at the age of twenty to prepare to become a rural clergyman.[65] In those studies, he was groomed theologically by a standard classroom text written by William Paley and entitled *Natural Theology; or Evidences of the Existence and Attributes of the Deity*.[66] In this widely used text, Paley argued that the beauty and harmony of the natural world gave evidence for the existence of a God who created everything that is. Paley was fond of using the analogy of a watch: If one comes upon a watch lying on the ground and examines it, one would be impressed by the complexity and integration of all of the parts working together to enable the watch to express time. One would never assume that there was not a watchmaker for

64. Greshko and National Geographic Staff, "What Are Mass Extinctions?"
65. Desmon and Moore, *Darwin*, 47–48.
66. Paley, *Natural Theology*.

such a watch to exist. Likewise, when one encounters the features of nature, one is impressed by their complexity and harmony and beauty. One would have to surmise that this reality, too, was made by a world-maker for such a world to exist. That world-maker is God.[67]

Darwin confesses that he did not question the premises of this argument from design for God's existence (the "teleological argument" in philosophy). "I did not trouble myself about Paley's premises; and taking these on trust, I was charmed and convinced by the long line of argumentation."[68]

Darwin completed his studies in 1831 and received his degree in theology but did not become a country parson. Instead, his curiosity about biological life drew him into a study of beetles, birds, lizards, and other species. Then, aided by the intervention of his uncle to gain Darwin's father's permission, he embarked on a five-year voyage on *HMS Beagle*, captained by Robert Fitzroy. That experience changed his life, for in his observation of the natural world he came to conclude that the earth was not six thousand years old, as Bishop James Ussher had calculated, and that species were not fixed over time but changed, adapted, evolved. His theory of evolution through the means of natural selection would revolutionize science by explaining the adaptation that characterized the variation he found in different environments.

The length of time that evolution required, and the macro-suffering that less-favored specimens underwent, forced him to raise questions about a literal interpretation of the creation stories in Genesis and the timeline of the Christian tradition's understanding up to that time of life on the planet and how it came to be.

Darwin came to recognize also the brutality of nature. Nature is not solely beautiful and harmonious, but also involves intense micro-suffering and death due to predation and parasitism. Foxes hunt, kill, and eat rabbits. Some wasps lay their eggs in the flesh of caterpillars, and these parasites are nourished at the expense of other living things by eating their flesh. Echoing Tennyson, nature was indeed "red in tooth and claw." This awareness contrasted the positive and sanitized "picture" of nature that Paley had painted and which predominated nineteenth-century theology.

Dr. Wayne Dyer, in his book *Your Erroneous Zones*, amplifies Darwin's recognition:

---

67. Paley, *Natural Theology*, 3, 261–62, 40, 441; Curry, *Children of God*, 27–28; cf. Charles Darwin, *Autobiography*, 56–71.

68. Charles Darwin, *Autobiography*, 59.

> The world is simply not put together [for justice]. Robins eat worms. That's not fair to the worms. Spiders eat flies. That's not fair to the flies. Cougars kill coyotes. Coyotes kill badgers. Badgers kill mice. Mice kill bugs.... You only have to look at nature to see that there is no justice in the world.[69]

Then Darwin's most acute experience of deep suffering and intense grief came from the death of his daughter, Annie, at the age of ten, most likely of tuberculosis (she had contracted scarlet fever two years before, along with two of her sisters). Darwin had ten children in all, and the precocious, curious-thinking, Anne Elizabeth ("the joy of the household," as Darwin described her in a memorial written days after her death), was unquestionably his favorite. Both Charles and his first-cousin wife, Emma, were devastated by Annie's death, and Charles never fully recovered from it.[70] The major theological vision of his time—God creating a beautiful world and God fully in charge of all the happenings therein—was repugnant to Darwin, and although he never completely forsook his faith, he became an agnostic (some would argue he became a deist, holding the view that God created the world but was no longer involved in it or directing it). He had no other viable theological model to which to turn.

A century before, Englishman John Newton (1725–1807), who penned the lyrics to the renowned hymn "Amazing Grace," was also a person who had distanced himself from his Christian faith when his mother, Elizabeth, died from tuberculosis when Newton was not quite seven years old. His mother had been a devout Christian, a "Dissenter" (or "Nonconformist," a religious group established outside the Anglican state church), who had exerted a tremendous spiritual influence on her son.[71] Although a severe storm that he experienced in 1748 while working on the slave ship *The Greyhound* marked his return to his Christian upbringing, his initial straying from faith should not be minimized.[72] As was the case with Darwin, Newton had had trouble reconciling the death of a loving, deeply Christian mother with a God who controlled or caused everything and seemed to take her from him through a debilitating disease.

In all of these sources from literature and history, from Camus to Newton, the conundrum has been how to understand a God who typically

---

69. Dyer, *Your Erroneous Zones*, 173.
70. Browne, *Charles Darwin*, 499, 501.
71. *Christianity Today*, "John Newton."
72. MacKim, "Amazing Grace."

and traditionally is the cause of all that happens—or in some cases, *allows* the things to happen that happen—and yet is affirmed as all-loving, all-good, all-knowing, and all-powerful. And the reconciliation of moral evil, perhaps quintessentially represented by the Holocaust in the case of Anne Frank and Elie Wiesel especially, and of natural evil—such as disease, typhoons, evolution, tornadoes, climate change, and floods—represented powerfully by Camus, Chaucer, Hart, Kushner, Tennyson, Darwin, and Newton, with a powerful, good, just, knowing, and loving God has been biblically analyzed by Anderson and Brueggemann and theologically suggested by Augustine.

But, as C. S. Lewis laments in terms of divine goodness, "If God's goodness is inconsistent with hurting us, then either God is not good or there is not God: For in the only life we know, He hurts us beyond our worst fears and beyond all we can imagine."[73] In *Night*, after witnessing babies being used for target practice, people digging their own graves, and victims burned in the crematoria while still alive, Wiesel proclaims, "I wasn't doubting [God's] existence, but I doubted God's absolute justice."[74] Also in *Night*, Akiba Drummer sees the suffering as a trial:

> God is testing us. He wants to see whether we are capable of overcoming our base instincts, of killing the Satan within ourselves. We have no right to despair, and if God punishes us mercilessly, it is a sign that God loves us that much more.[75]

God's goodness is questioned; God's justice is questioned; God's love is expressed as punishment. What is not questioned is God's power.

Thus, God caused or allowed the premature death of a loved one . . . the lonely demise of an elderly parent from COVID in a hospital with no visitors allowed . . . or a rape . . . or the abduction of a young, seven-year-old girl by a FedEx driver who then murdered her . . . or the freezing of pipes at a food bank which caused one million dollars of foodstuffs for the homeless to be ruined?

All these events—(a) Were they in accord with God's will because God "sent" or caused them (as punishment for sin and/or to teach us a lesson)? (b) Were they not in accord with God's will, but God did not interfere in order to preserve human freedom of choice or to allow natural processes

---

73. Lewis, *Grief Observed*, 27.
74. Wiesel, *Night*, 45.
75. Wiesel, *Night*, 45.

to run their course? (c) Did God not interfere because God is not a good or benevolent deity, but instead not just a cosmic Dictator but a cosmic Sadist? (d) Does God struggle against another cosmic force—Satan, the devil, Lucifer, Beelzebub—and this malevolent power caused the "bad things" to occur? (e) Did God not interfere because God is weak and could not do so? (f) Do we need to recognize that God's ways are shrouded in mystery, so we do not/cannot know the answer, but we can choose to have strong faith nevertheless? (g) Is God remote and therefore not involved in the situations and comings and goings of life and events in the world?

Chapter Five

An Alternative Vision of God

If God controls everything, then the buck stops at the divine desk: Every incidental thing—no matter how large or miniscule—comes into existence via the power and providence of God, the direct hand of Almighty God.

I recall sitting in a cancer ward at a hospital, awaiting the negative outcome of an oncology appointment involving my friend "Sheila": The diagnosis was that Sheila had cancer. Did God send that cancer? Permit that cancer? Tolerate cancer as the diabolical activity of a demonic force opposed to God? Allow cancer as the operation of natural forces that are not benign?

If/since God *sent* it, then Sheila deserved the cancer? She had committed sins—as all humans do—and this came as punishment for that sin? What sin would have been sufficient to warrant a woman's harrowing affliction with breast cancer?

Did God *allow* her to get cancer? That is, God could have prevented her contraction of it (since God is all-powerful, therefore can do anything, and is in control of everything that happens), but for some reason elected not to do so? Sheila chose to smoke (she didn't), so getting lung cancer would be the result of poor human judgment (but she had *breast* cancer!)? Thus, this is not divine judgment, rather it is the just consequence of fallacious decisions and regrettable human actions? Therefore, it is the judgment of nature (if you pollute your body with carcinogens, then you pay the health price?!)?

Or did the devil send cancer to afflict Sheila? The devil, in "a cosmic struggle with God and in an intimate dance with us humans,"[1] is the source of all bad things? In this case, these maladies do not come from God (though God could prevent or abrogate them if God so chose), but from a powerful anti-good Force that brings things to cause suffering, especially of God's children, in order, perhaps, to dissuade persons from maintaining their belief and thus causing them to lose it. But, since God is truly and finally in charge, God allows this as a "test of faith": Will persons continue to believe and to have faith? If they will, then their faith will become even stronger, the way that heat galvanizes metal.

Or, is God an "absentee landlord" who is not present to prevent the contraction of cancer? Did God create the world and the natural laws that operate within it, but now watches it from afar—with the satisfaction of One who created something out of nothing—and gazes upon its operation without divine involvement? That means that if a baby were to fall from a great height (the notorious example of the late Michael Jackson dangling his son over a balcony in a hotel in Germany twenty years ago comes to mind), then nature's law of gravity would guarantee the baby's injury and, most likely, death. God, then, is not involved in the creation as a cause in the world on a regular basis, but only as a "First Cause" that initially created "what is." This point of view preserves the doctrine of creation in the Christian tradition—the existence and the power of God (and God's goodness, since, according to the account in Gen 1, the creation is *tov*, good)—but it evaporates the doctrine of providence—the affirmation that God continues to act in the world that God created.[2]

But could God still intervene "from afar" if the situation warranted it? In the Bible, "miracles" appear as suspensions of natural law—a person is brought back to life from death, the people of Israel escape sure capture when a body of water "parts" or "divides" so that they may not be captured and most likely killed, a hungry crowd by the Sea of Galilee is fed with initially insufficient amounts of fish and loaves, a religious figure—Jesus, then temporarily, Peter—walks on water, etc. So, even a "remote God" *could* intervene when the situation calls for it. Thus, when the situation warrants it, God ceases being an absentee landlord momentarily and steps

---

1. Spinney, *Pale Rider*, 284.
2. *Continua creatio* is the Latin phrase theologians use to refer to this.

AN ALTERNATIVE VISION OF GOD

in to adjust things and make corrections. An analogy is a grandfather clock in my dining room: I set the time, I pull the chains to elevate the weights, and the clock runs on its own. Occasionally, I must take action to step in and adjust the time, and each week I must reset the weights. But normally, typically, daily, it runs on its own.[3]

The strength of this theological "move" is to remove God from direct causation and direct responsibility. God is no longer the meticulous meddler of the Middle Ages, whose anger is provoked by human failings and foul-ups and whose actions in history and nature result in tremendous happenings and terrible punishments.

This was the position of a number of the Founding Fathers of America, whose "deistic" theologies were a way of reconciling their God-concept and their faith systems with the rational analysis and understanding of the world birthed by the Enlightenment and bolstered by the advent of science in the seventeenth, eighteenth, and nineteenth centuries. Thomas Jefferson and his self-edited Bible (the "Jefferson Bible") are but one notable example.[4]

It was also the position of Jewish scientist and philosopher Albert Einstein, who, though he still believed in God, conceived of that God as a Prime Mover or Initial Cause who brought things into being, but then watches from afar. Einstein said that the personal, biblical God would not "fit" into a world understood by science. Instead, he referred to a Cosmic Cause, the Unmoved Mover, who was responsible for the creation, but no longer plays a role in it. For Einstein, God is totally transcendent and no longer engaged in the world, save perhaps through the natural laws that regulate how life evolved and how things go on planet Earth.

The century before, Charles Darwin had given up his belief in a personal God who was active in the world. The evolution of species on Earth had taken an almost unfathomable length of time, thus debunking the belief in a "young Earth," and natural selection produced extraordinary suffering among life forms on the planet.

> From death, famine, rapine, and the concealed war of nature, we can see that the highest good, which we can conceive, the creation of the higher animals has come.[5]

---

3. Theologian Ted Peters makes use of a similar analogy in his insightful book, *Playing God*.

4. Blakemore, "Why Thomas Jefferson Rewrote."

5. Francis Darwin, "Two Essays Written in 1842 and 1844," in *Foundations of the*

In his *Autobiography*, Darwin indicates again his difficulty in the traditional concept of God:

> The old argument from design in nature, as given by Paley, which formerly seemed to me so conclusive, fails, now that the law of natural selection has been discovered.[6]

As has been noted in the previous chapter, when he experienced the death of his daughter Annie, in 1851 at the age of ten, his faith was punctured: His experience no longer permitted him to believe in the omnipotent, omniscient, and omnibenevolent God that Paley described, for which there had been seemingly convincing proof in the beauty, complexity, harmony, and order of the natural world. Darwin no longer saw God as good, nor did he picture God as acting in benevolent ways in the world. Instead, God was the all-powerful First Cause that brought things into being, but did not care about nor care for the world that had been created.

Darwin's concept of a personal God was "dead." *God* was not necessarily dead, but that *concept* of God was no longer feasible, applicable, and persuasive to him. The Judeo-Christian tradition had affirmed an all-powerful God who *does* act in the world, a God who *can* and *does* intervene in the causal nexus of things when it has gotten too bad and/or is so far out of conformity to God's preference, God's will, that a correction must be made. So, *if* God had the unlimited power to intervene and prevent such evil things from happening, *why* did God not do so? In other words, why did God permit to happen what God had the power to prohibit from happening? Or, since/if God had the power to jump in and at least *mitigate* the breadth and depth of a tragedy, why did God not at least do *this*? Darwin found that the concept of an all-powerful, loving, and good God did not jibe with his experience in a world of natural selection and the death of a child, his beloved daughter.

In a certain sense, this is an echo of Friedrich Nietzsche's proclamation in *Thus Spoke Zarathustra* that "God was dead."[7] Nietzsche did not mean metaphysically that God did not exist, but rather, that the prevalent concept of God was no longer widely enough accepted to give meaning to human life. "God 'dies' when there is no good reason to believe that

---

Origin of Species, 52 (at the end of the 1842 essay).

6. Charles Darwin, *Autobiography*, 87.

7. Nietzsche, *Thus Spoke Zarathustra*, 1; he also mentioned the death of God in the book preceding *Thus Spoke Zarathustra*, *Gay Science*, sections 108, 125.

God exists."[8] In other words, belief in the traditional God-concept of the monotheistic faiths had become unbelievable then, and, in light of pandemics such as COVID and horrors such as the Holocaust, now. It is no longer tenable to believe that we suffer, either because we always deserve it or because it is the irrevocable and irresistible result of the human abuse of authentic freedom or nature's unassailable terror, about which God in God's mystery chooses to do nothing.

If God does *not* intervene, then the situation must not have called for it. Since God did not intervene (if God could actually do so if God wanted) in the case of Sheila's breast cancer, in the case of Darwin's daughter, in Anne Frank's capture by the Gestapo, then that situation did not warrant it. And why not?

God alone knows! But, since God is mysterious and God's ways are far removed from human ways, God must have had an incomprehensible reason for not intervening.

> For my thoughts are not your thoughts, nor are your ways my ways, says the Lord. For as the heavens are higher than the earth, so are my ways higher than your ways, and my thoughts than your thoughts. (Isa 55:8–9)
>
> The secret things belong to the Lord our God ... (Deut 29:29a)
>
> How unsearchable are God's judgments and how inscrutable God's ways! For who has known the mind of the Lord? (Rom 11:33b–34a)

These humbling passages certainly acknowledge the majesty and sovereignty of God and preserve the distance between humans and God. Human beings are *not* God, and only pride (*hubris*) would account for humans believing that they *are* God. At the same time, the passages justify God at the expense of human experience in the case of the onslaught of cancer in Sheila's life. Since we cannot know the reason why God did not intervene—because God's ways are inscrutable, secret, and not our ways—then God's power and goodness are preserved, but at the expense of the human experience of suffering from disease and human reflection upon it.

It is time. It is beyond time to let go, to let go of this traditional image of an all-powerful God who controls everything or permits everything, and whose actions and purposes, shrouded in mystery, are unavailable

---

8. Remhof, "'God is dead.'"

and unassailable to human comprehension. That concept is no longer relevant and persuasive. As actor Morgan Freeman said as Professor Harry Scott in the 2007 film *Feast of Love*, "God either is dead or despises us."[9] If God is dead, then all of what happens to us—the good and the bad—just happens, by chance, coincidence, or natural causes; consequently, there is no divine help, no power greater than ours to rely on and to provide hope. But if God is alive, then an all-powerful deity must hate humans because of what that God does to us. As Jewish philosopher Hans Jonas (1903–93) has put it, "After Auschwitz we can no longer believe in the omnipotence of God."[10] Richard Rubenstein makes the point even more strongly, "After Auschwitz there can be no belief in God whatsoever." Here Rabbi Rubenstein denies both an omnipotent and benevolent God: There is no all-powerful God who manipulates human behavior like a puppeteer dangling marionettes, and there is no all-good and all-powerful God who safeguards the Chosen People. Thus, there is no cosmos-controlling God.[11] Holocaust survivor Primo Levi puts it more succinctly: "There is Auschwitz. And so, there cannot be God."[12]

That is, *if* the classical concept of God as all-powerful, all-knowing, all-loving, and all-present is *the* model for divine Reality. Traditionally, God must be omnipotent, omniscient, omnibenevolent, and omnipresent in order to "be" God. But COVID-19 and other pandemics, as well as the Holocaust and many lesser evils, call that into question. Is the only option to believe in the notion of a Cosmic Autocrat or become an atheist?[13]

Or, can the experience of the latest pandemic (COVID), and the recollection of a distant horror (the Holocaust) serve as a portal into another world?

> Nothing could be worse than a return to normality. Historically, pandemics have forced humans to break with the past and imagine their world anew. This one is no different. It is a portal, a gateway between one world and the next. We can choose to walk through it [carrying our old carcasses of dead ideas] . . . . Or

---

9. Benton, *Feast of Love*.

10. Vogel, *Mortality and Morality* (a collection of articles on the thought of Hans Jonas), quoted in Karen Armstrong, *History of God*, 381.

11. Rubenstein, *After Auschwitz*.

12. Levi, quoted in Click, "Elie Wiesel's Unique Journey," 8.

13. Theologian Catherine Keller alludes to this dilemma in "Gallop of the Pale Green Horse," 41–42.

we can walk through lightly with little luggage ready to imagine another world.[14]

Is God the Master of the Universe, or more like a Tender of the Garden?[15] Is God King ruling over us or is God Kin working with us? Does God act in the world by utilizing the proverbial stick to bludgeon us for going the wrong way or by utilizing a carrot to entice us to go in the right direction? Is God's power more like a vise to squeeze us into conformity with God's will or more like a magnet to attract us to doing God's will? The former of each of these pairs is a classical theistic model based on absolute control; the latter is a different model based on "another world," a different concept of God. Our traditional concept of God needs to change in order to account for phenomena such as pandemics and holocausts, for all instances of natural evil and the horrors of moral evil.

Over sixty years ago, the bishop of Woolwich, England—John A. T. Robinson—wrote in his book *Honest to God* of a revolution that needed to happen in the way we understood God. This revolution, he reflected, would question the orthodox doctrinal assumptions that the church and many Christians had firmly held and widely promulgated for a very long period of time. In short, he observed that the concept of God as only "up there" (as the "old Man in the sky") and "out there" (as an aloof Judge) needed to be jettisoned and "radically recast" in favor of an immanent God who loves us, who is steadfastly with us, who immeasurably cares about us, and who unquestionably forgives us.[16]

He predicted that his book would be considered radical and perhaps even heretical, but he assured the reader that it was "honest"—for he took seriously the gap between what traditional orthodox supernaturalist theology tenaciously held onto and what the public was experiencing and how it was reflecting on that experience. He elected to close that gap by accenting the contributions of theologian Paul Tillich in locating God in the depth of our lives, as the Ground of Being.

Robinson noted that the God "up there" (occupying the top level of a three-story universe) was replaced by the God "out there," when the

---

14. Roy, "Pandemic Is a Portal," quoted in Keller, "Gallop of the Pale Green Horse," 47–48.

15. Both Ian Barbour and Catherine Keller use the image of "God as Gardener" or "Sower of Seeds," respectively, in Barbour, *Religion in an Age of Science*, 176; and Keller, "Gallop of the Pale Green Horse," 50.

16. Robinson, *Honest to God*, 7.

multi-layered worldview became obsolete.[17] But this was not enough, he contended, for rather than being a helpful innovation, it simply repackaged the God "up there" as the God "out there." As a result, he "relocated" God as the "Beyond in the midst of life" (the phrase is from German theologian and martyr Dietrich Bonhoeffer).[18]

Bishop Robinson went on to suggest that for some the denial of a God "out there"—but now "in here" as the Ground of Being, as the Beyond in the midst of life—might be considered a denial of God altogether.[19] But such inflexible recalcitrance is not necessary, he said, for our concept of God, our understanding of the Divine, has never been static, but has been historically in flux.

Theologian Paul Tillich reminded us that our concept of God falls way short of totally encapsulating the reality of God. At best, our God-concept at any particular time—whatever that specific time—is merely a "symbol" for God. But just as a symbol (like the national flag or a wedding ring or the Christian cross) participates in the reality to which it points, that gives us information, that says something significant, about God. But it does not indicate everything about God. That is, what we think about God is a metaphor for God. We take what we can know—human thoughts and human characteristics—and utilize them to describe God. In so doing, we must acknowledge that the reality we are attempting to describe is always greater than the concepts and words we use. Just as a human person is more than words can describe, so much more is our concept of God incapable of a full and accurate description of the actual reality of God.

Photography might serve as an example of this: If God in God's full and accurate reality could be represented as a color photograph, then our thoughts about God are, at best, a black and white photograph; some might even argue a caricature such as those created by artists at street fairs. Some of the details of God's nature are discernible, but the complete vision of God is only partially discernible and eludes complete discovery.[20]

But, again, this does not mean that we cannot come to any knowledge at all about God. Knowing another person fully is never possible;

---

17. Robinson, *Honest to God*, 13–18.

18. Bonhoeffer, *Letters and Papers from Prison*, 282 (the letter is to Eberhard Bethge and dates from April 30, 1944); cf. Münchow, "'God Is the Beyond.'"

19. Robinson, *Honest to God*, 17.

20. This photography example was suggested by Daniel Migliore in *Faith Seeking Understanding*, 20ff.

AN ALTERNATIVE VISION OF GOD

but knowing significant information about him/her is possible and is absolutely necessary, especially if we desire to be in an intimate, trusting relationship. Thus it is with God. Though we cannot know God fully (and theologian Karl Barth indicates that we only know what we know about God, because God has revealed that to us—and what God has revealed to us is that God is mysterious!), we know enough about the Divine Mystery to be able to trust, to obey, and to follow.

Since the true reality of God can only be approximated, our mental picture of God can change. As experiences accumulate and insights emerge, that concept *must* change in order to become cogent and to remain relevant. Robert Wright, in his insightful seminal work, *The Evolution of God*, delineates some of the important ways our God-concept has changed (he would say, "evolved") over time. Originally, Divinity was understood pluralistically: There were many gods, oftentimes representations of the various forces of nature—a sun god, a rain god, a storm god, a lightning god, fertility god(s), etc. Such polytheism has been acknowledged as the oldest understanding of Divinity, originating thousands of years ago. When the Israelites began their cultural and religious journey, they were at first polytheistic, acknowledging the pantheon of gods commonly recognized. Indeed, even upon arrival in the promised land, the "land flowing with milk and honey," they recognized multiple gods and, because the nomads necessarily became farmers, they flirted with, and worshiped, agricultural deities such as Baal and Ashtart, who stayed put and took care of the farm. Better to cover all the bases beyond allegiance to the mobile warrior god, Yahweh (the Lord), who had liberated them from Egyptian bondage and delivered them at the "Red Sea" and led them into the land of Canaan!

Eventually, they would swear off the worship of other gods in favor of their tribal deity, Yahweh. They did not cease to believe in multiple gods but devoted themselves to the worship of one of them. This could be likened to persons' loyalty and dedication to the Carolina Panthers football team while acknowledging the existence of a number of other professional teams in the NFL. Scholars refer to this position and posture as "henotheism."

By the watershed time of the exile and return following the Babylonians' victory over the Israelites in the sixth century BCE, and then the return facilitated by King Cyrus of Persia, the Israelites changed and evolved to monotheism, the recognition that Yahweh was not just one god among many, but the only god there was. This was the first firm occupation of the position of "monotheism."[21]

What is clear here is not that God in God's actual reality had fluctuated over time, but rather that human perception of God had altered as situations and times had changed and new insights emerged. As scholar Karen Armstrong has suggested, any particular idea of God must—if it is to survive—*work* for the people who develop it and live by it. Ideas of God modify when they cease to be effective. She continues by observing that the ever-changing ideas of God have led us to our time, and that we must begin to envision a new concept of God in the twenty-first century. Her book, then, is a history of the way humans have perceived God from Abraham to the present time.[22]

Born a Muslim, converting to Christianity, then returning to Islam again, scholar Reza Aslan recalls that when he was a little boy,

> I thought God was a large, powerful old man who lived in the sky—a bigger, stronger version of my father, but with magical powers. I imagined him handsome and grizzled, his long gray hair draped over his broad shoulders. He sat on a throne enwrapped by clouds, when he spoke his voice boomed through the heavens, especially when he was angry. And he was often angry. But he was also warm and loving, merciful and kind. He laughed when he was happy and cried when he was sad.[23]

Journalist and former Jesuit Jack Miles, in *God: A Biography*, which won the Pulitzer Prize for biography or autobiography, creatively treats God as a literary figure in the Bible.[24] In this treatment, God's character changes within the narrative of the Hebrew Bible (Christian Old Testament). Miles argues that God has a complex and ever-changing personality as the "hero" of the Hebrew Bible and changes from the energetic Creator (a sort of Michelangelo's David) to a sedate Ancient of Days (a William Blake's white-haired deity) by the end.

Professor Miles's book is not so much a tome about theology as it is about the creative way in which Bible writers reflect (or have revealed to them) the various characteristics of God. As reviewer Paul Johnson notes, polytheism has many gods with each possessing a salient characteristic.

21. Robert Wright, *Evolution of God*, 17, 71, 150, 101.
22. Karen Armstrong, *History of God*, xviii–xxiii, 377–99.
23. Aslan, *God*, xi.
24. Miles, *God*.

Monotheism, by contrast, has one God embodying all the various aspects of divinity. "God has to play all the parts."[25]

What is significant is not whether Professor Miles provides an accurate picture of God, but rather the observation that the picture of God can change through time in light of unanticipated events, life-changing crises, cultural changes, scientific discoveries, and unimaginable breakthroughs.

The COVID-19 pandemic has been one of the unique experiences of our lives. COVID has not just changed a few things, it changed everything—from our way of relating, to our way of working, to our way of worshiping, to our sense of invulnerability, to our frequency and confidence in traveling, to our way of teaching and of learning, to a new anxiety of helplessness, to questioning how we love our neighbors by what we do (to mask or not to mask), to trusting science (to vaccinate or not to vaccinate). As Bishop N. T. Wright put it in his book *God and the Pandemic*, "There hasn't been a moment like this in my lifetime."[26]

And as has been noted previously, COVID has raised theological questions about our understanding of God. What is God's connection to COVID? What is the relationship of God and God's love and God's power and God's action to COVID deaths and to the suffering caused by its onslaught? Did God send this pandemic upon us for some divine reason? Did God permit the disease to afflict us for some purpose? Was God unable to prevent it or to mitigate it? What is God's "job description" in our lives? What does God "do" in the world?

And as has also been noted before, the Holocaust has raised theological questions about our "picture" of God. What is God's connection to one of the most diabolical and tragic events of the last century, the murder of six million Jews and four to five million more persons who were "different," ostracized and then systematically killed? How can an image and belief in an all-powerful, all-knowing, and all-good God withstand the onslaught of the annihilation of these human beings and the suffering caused to them and to countless others? Did God punish these persons by either causing or allowing the Holocaust? Was God too anemic to keep it from happening or to lessen its depth and breadth of pain and horror? How does God act in our lives? What is God "up to" in the world?

Traditionally, these questions were "answered"—or at least, addressed—by the doctrine of providence (*providēre*, Latin for "to provide

25. Paul Johnson, Review of *God: A Biography*.
26. N. T. Wright, *God and the Pandemic*, 43.

for" or "to supply") in theology. That is, the doctrine of providence is the theological category that presents "how God provides for God's people as God guides them in their journey of faith through life, accomplishing God's divine purpose in them."[27] The notion of God's providence—God's presence and God's care—has given people hope and courage and strength in dealing with the difficulties and challenges of life.

But how was God present and caring in COVID, how was God involved in this pandemic? And how was God involved in the two previous pandemics discussed, the fourteenth-century bubonic plague and the twentieth-century Spanish flu? And, for that matter, how was God involved in mass atrocities such as the Holocaust and the singular example of Anne Frank, and the horrible death of a single child, whether from disease, like Rabbi Harold Kushner's son, or due to abduction and murder?

In response to this question, and as we have seen, some theologians and religious leaders have simply fallen back on old assumptions and familiar tenets and confidently reasserted the pious platitudes of the past: Accordingly, it is insisted and declared that God is in total control of everything that happens, and therefore COVID-19 and the Holocaust in some way, and ultimately, occurred by God's power and will and served God's purpose and plan, now and in the end. And though it is impossible for us humans ever to understand God and God's ways fully, God's righteousness punishes us for our sins as a deserved judgment or teaches us a lesson to thereby prompt our repentance or tests our faith by checking our resilience or propels us to evangelize more intentionally and more thoroughly or alerts us to the end time and its unavoidable final judgment. God's purpose, God's will, God's intention could include two or more of these goals.

But what if God is *not* in control of everything that happens? What if God does not cause or allow natural maladies and acts of individual or collective moral wickedness? What, then, would God's job description be in the world? What would God *do*? For what would God be responsible? What difference would God make? What difference would belief in God make?

---

27. Llanes, "Theology Thursday: God's Providence."

Chapter Six

Love as the Primary Divine Characteristic

WE FREQUENTLY USE PARENTAL, symbolic language to speak of God—God is our "father" a "Father who art in heaven" (the opening of the Lord's Prayer in Matt 6:9 and Luke 11:2). "I believe in God the Father Almighty, Maker of heaven and earth" (the Apostles' Creed). Plus, Jesus calls God *Abba*, or "Daddy," an Aramaic word that denotes deep intimacy and a compassionate, caring relationship.

As a part of the parental upbringing of children, a father or mother will allow his/her child to make choices, some of which may not be in the child's best and healthiest interest. That is the way children learn—they choose, and some of those choices are not good ones, and they can learn from their mistakes (but not guaranteed). In her diary, Anne Frank writes, "Parents can only advise their children or point them in the right direction. Ultimately, people shape their own characters."[1] Her father, Otto, agreed, she adds, when he noted, "every child has to raise itself."[2]

But, if a child is going to choose to do something truly unwise, or really stupid, or patently illegal, or irreversibly lethal, the mother or father will forcefully intervene—so much is at stake that the intervention is justified. If

1. Frank, *Diary of a Young Girl*, 355.
2. Frank, *Diary of a Young Girl*, 355.

a parent does not step forward to hold the child's hand from his/her choosing to cross the street recklessly and thereby walk into oncoming traffic, we would regard that parent as irresponsible, not as a good and loving parent. If a child wanders down the path of drug usage, what parent would not orchestrate an intervention and get her/his child into specialized care? If a parent declined to do so, or even more egregiously, refused to do so, we would evaluate that parent as unloving, uncaring, and "unfit."

When I was very young and being reared by a single-parent mother, my babysitter, "Lori," looked after me and safeguarded me from danger. One day the two of us approached the main street of town and waited for the traffic light to change so that we might cross the street. Impatient and oblivious to the risk, I slipped my hand out of hers and started to bolt across the street, right into the path of an approaching car. I recall distinctly that Lori took some very quick steps and grabbed me by my shoulders and jerked me back out of harm's way.

She had the power to do this, so she did it! She did not let my human freedom to choose to do something stupid—perhaps lethal—keep her from saving me from injury and very likely death. No one could or would question her intention and courage. *Not* to do what she did would have been irresponsible; indeed, her inaction would have made her culpable for my injury or death.

Why is it not the same way in our understanding of God?

If God has the power to interrupt a process that has gone too far in a bad way or to prevent a terrible event from happening, why would God not do so? To appeal to mystery—i.e., we just don't know the answer to this question, because we *cannot* penetrate the mystery of God and understand God's ways—lets God off the hook at the expense of human experience. It is not a satisfactory theological response to our pain and suffering, for it might mean that human suffering serves some sort of divine purpose; or it could mean that God is nasty, not nice, and evil—God could be a cosmic Sadist rather than a divine Lover. If God could have prevented the Holocaust—or at least reduced its severity—and chose not to do so, what kind of God would have failed to act? If God could have prevented the onslaught of COVID-19 and the disproportionate deaths of elderly persons—and chose not to do so, what kind of God would have failed to do so?

And interpreting that pain and suffering as *caused* by God—rather than just *permitted* by God—makes our picture of God even more uncomfortable and ominous in light of divine wrath. Ultimately, from this perspective,

God becomes the Author of human sin (whatever happens is God's will, and human freedom to choose is actually an illusion), the Dictator of horrific events (as God's punishment for that sin, inconsistently if humans do not have genuine freedom), the Educator who sends pain and suffering to teach us something important and to strengthen our souls (but if we die from it, what is the lesson taught and learned? That God is malevolent?).

On the other hand, perhaps God does not have the power to intervene in all situations that warrant it. Perhaps it unsettles and upsets God that God cannot do so. If a child dies, and God did not have the power to prevent that death, then God "cries" along with the parents—in fact, the parents most likely were doing everything they possibly could to prevent that death. God was, too.

If God "cries tears" along with the parents—though God *could* have prevented the child's death—then aren't those tears insincere, even phony (the way some people at a funeral do not know well the deceased or even the survivors but nevertheless feel obligated to manifest pain to, and even cry tears with, the bereaved)?

So, divine tears are an expression that God could not do something to reverse the situation. If God *could* have done so, God, because of God's love, *would* have done so. But that does not mean that God was not involved. God was doing all that God could do. But God's power is persuasive, not coercive; God's action is passionately suggestive, not fully controlling.

In regard to the traffic situation with my babysitter, God was not directly controlling or determining what happened. Though God was undoubtedly appealing to me not to break free from Lori and run toward the traffic, I was oblivious to, or simply ignored, that divine action. God did not save me singlehandedly; God was stimulating my babysitter to take the action that would spare me. If I had been killed, God would not have caused it. If I had been killed, God would not have permitted it. God was doing all God could do to keep me from harm. Lori responded and reached out and grabbed me. If she had not done so, when she had the opportunity and the power to do so, she would have been held accountable for my injury and, likely, my death.

What this means for pandemics is that God suffered with victims of COVID (and of the bubonic plague and of the Spanish flu), and God struggled with helping them regain health. But God did not send the pandemic, cause them to become stricken with the virus, and then shed tears when they suffered because it was God's will that they became infected.

No, God was genuinely saddened, deeply suffered, and wished it were otherwise; for God did not impose the pandemic as God's will for that person and for the world.

In fact, theologian Dietrich Bonhoeffer, martyred by the Nazis in 1945 for his part in an assassination plot against Hitler, said that God's action must be seen through the filter of the cross (God suffering in Jesus for us and with us). He made the point that God decided to enter the world as a helpless babe in a manger, so God acts in the world in helplessness and weakness.[3] Although Bonhoeffer did not erase the ultimate power that God possessed, he suggested that God's majesty lay not in God's overwhelming power, but in God's steadfast love.

> God is weak and powerless in the world, and that is precisely the way, the only way, in which God is with us and helps us. Matthew 8:17 makes it quite clear that Christ helps us, not by virtue of his omnipotence, but by virtue of his weakness and suffering.[4]

Theologian Jürgen Moltmann, in his famous book, *The Crucified God*, also points to the cross of Jesus as the paradigm through which to view and understand the action of God in the world.

> The death of Jesus on the Cross is the center of all Christian theology. All Christian statements about God, about creation, about sin and death have their focal point in the crucified Christ.[5]

Thus, God's power must be understood as the power to accomplish something good out of suffering and weakness, though God did *not* cause that suffering or weakness, or did not choose not to intervene to do something to prevent it. God does not work through force or by bludgeoning. "The cross is God's alternative to the sword."[6]

---

3. Bonhoeffer, *Letters and Papers from Prison*, 279; Duchemin, "Bonhoeffer's Concept of the Weakness of God," 1–15: Though some biblical texts refer to God's overwhelming power (Exod 19:16; Deut 4:34), other texts refer to "the way of weakness" as a means to overcome "inimical forces" (1 Sam 2:4; Isa 40:29; 1 Kgs 19:12; Judg 7:1–7). Since the advent of Christ, God chooses the way of weakness. Of course, for Bonhoeffer, God could have chosen otherwise and been fully in control. However, here we are arguing that God acts in the way of loving weakness because that is God's only option. God lovingly tries to persuade us to do the good; God is not coercively dictating the outcome.

4. Bonhoeffer, *Letters and Papers from Prison*, 360.
5. Quoted in Zahnd, "Crucified God."
6. Zahnd, "Crucified God."

This might allow for a more helpful interpretation of the scene, which we have considered previously, in Elie Wiesel's *Night* in which the young boy is hanged in the concentration camp. His weight is insufficient to cause his immediate death, so he twitches at the end of the rope for what seemed to the inmates to be an eternity. And someone in the crowd yells out the question, "Where is God?" From within himself, Wiesel hears another voice, "There, God is there on the gallows."[7]

This scene has led many to the interpretive conclusion that God is dead, that God (or at least persons' faith in God) died with the young boy. But through the lens of Moltmann's proclamation, it could be understood that God did not cease to exist because of the suffering of the young boy, but, because God did not cause that suffering, God is identifying with the young man's suffering. In that sense, God was there on the gallows.

And if God identified with the boy's suffering but had the power to have prevented it in the first place, that is not a lack of activity of a *loving* God. If God could have prevented that tragedy, but chose to do nothing about it, then God's sympathy or empathy with the situation was superficial or worse, illusional. For if God truly could have intervened but did not do so in order that God could only suffer with the victim, then God would not seem to be loving. A loving God who had the power to stop that from happening surely would have done so. Thus, it would seem that God is either not loving or not all-powerful.

To say that God caused the suffering is to make God the source of evils such as the Holocaust and COVID-19 (and the bubonic plague and the Spanish flu). God's overwhelming power is preserved, but at the expense of God's goodness. To say that God allowed the suffering is to maintain once again God's omnipotence (God could have intervened, but for some reason elected not to do so), but at the expense of God's love.

Relatedly, theologian Thomas Jay Oord suggests seven models in Christian theology for understanding God's actions in the world:

> God is the "omnicause" (God is the only cause of all things and is in complete control);
>
> God grants free will to humans but sometimes overrides human freedom or "interrupts the causal regularities" of life in the world;

---

7. Wiesel, *Night*, 65.

God voluntarily limits God's power—God "*could* momentarily overturn the regularities/natural laws of the universe," but rarely chooses to do so;

God is "kenotic," meaning God's love is uncontrolling and that God empowers and inspires, but does not dictate;

God is an impersonal force that creates and sustains creation, but God is not personal and interactive with that creation;

God is an absentee landlord—God created the universe, but "did not stick around or stay involved";

God's reality and actions are shrouded in mystery—"God's ways are not our ways."[8]

Of these options, he holds to the fourth conception, but with a very important qualification—God's nature is primarily characterized by love, and for love *truly* to be love, it must not be coercive, it must do what it can to help, and it does not cause horrific pain, tremendous suffering, and uncaring death. Beyond this, for Dr. Oord, God's way of being and acting is such that God could not *choose* to be otherwise; in fact, God did not choose to be *this* way. Rather, it is simply God's *nature* to be this way.

In fact, Dr. Oord argues convincingly that God's love is the primary divine characteristic: "Love comes first, and this priority matters for understanding divine power."[9] Scripture attests to this—"For God so loved the world that God sent God's only Son" (John 3:16), and "God is love, and those who love, abide in God and God abides in them" (1 John 4:8, 16).

Further, here Christology (our understanding of Jesus) illumines theology (our understanding of God): Jesus's entire life and ministry were characterized by sacrificial love (*agapé*), and his willingness to include all others—even undesirables and those ostracized and marginalized by the society of his time—and to forgive his executioners while unjustly dying on a ghastly instrument of death instituted by the Romans (crucifixion), points to this love. He once proclaimed, "Greater love has no person than the one who is willing to lay down his life for his friends" (John 15:13).

If/since love is the primary characteristic of God, then God's power must be subsumed and understood in light of divine love. Love is the filter through which God's power is to be understood, and not vice versa. And

---

8. Oord, "Models of God's Action"; see Oord, *Uncontrolling Love of God*; *Death of Omnipotence*; *God Can't*.

9. Oord, *Death of Omnipotence*, 7.

what does "loving-power" or "powerful-loving" look like? It is not all-controlling and domineering. Instead, it operates by persuasion, not coercion; by luring, not dominating. As theologian Daniel Migliore has proclaimed, "If we attend closely to its story, the Bible subverts and transforms our conventional understandings of power."[10] Jesus has power "with" persons—not power "over" persons—and this is because his *agapé* love is enticingly (but not irresistibly) attractive. Jesus's love compels not by absolute force, but by invitation. He embodies love, he extends love; and this love appeals to others to emulate it:[11] To be a follower of Jesus is to choose to love because Jesus did so, and to understand that life has meaning because of that choice.

This focus on Jesus is what makes Christian theology *Christian*. Using Christ as the lens through which to understand God and God's power and God's love ("the Word became flesh and dwelt among us"—John 1:14a) distinguishes Christian theology from other religions' theologies. This means that our perception of who God is and what God is like and what God does is informed primarily by the person and work of Jesus of Nazareth. What we know about God we know through knowing Jesus.

Returning to Dr. Oord's seven options, in terms of the first option, God is perceived as totally in control; God exerts all power. However, this not only makes God singly responsible for every instance of suffering and evil, it also evaporates human freedom. If God determines everything, how can persons be responsible for their actions? According to this option, any apparent human freedom is an illusion, and if anyone concludes that s/he is an agent of moral choice, that is merely a delusion. As theologian Anna Case-Winters opines, "When God is seen as totally in control, any credible concepts of freedom and autonomy for human beings is relinquished, and human actions lose their significance."[12]

But if one nevertheless illogically asserts that God's "omnicausality" (i.e., God controls and causes everything) and human freedom are still maintained in the schematic of rewards for the righteous and punishments for the sinner, then how extreme do pain and suffering have to be not to be "covered" by this interpretation? Looking to the sins of the Jewish people (for, as the apostle Paul reminds all persons in Rom 3:23, "everyone sins and falls short of the glory of God") as justification for the horrible suffering that was levied on them, presupposes the relevance

---

10. Migliore, *Power of God*, 41.
11. Cf. Ritschl, *Christian Doctrine of Justification*.
12. Case-Winters, *God's Power*, 9.

and applicability of the ancient Deuteronomistic formula—"bad things happen to bad people and good things happen to good people"—to their murder. But what sin or set of sins would warrant such a systematic, efficient, and relentless attempted extermination of an entire people? and the killing of senior citizens? and the "weeding out" of the handicapped? and the forced labor (*Arbeit Macht Frei* on the gates of camps such as Auschwitz and Dachau) that worked persons to death before gassing them? and the murder of babies used for target practice?

Where is the "justice" here? From a moral perspective, sin should be punished, and righteousness rewarded. Sometimes they *are*; sometimes they are *not*. But from a theological perspective, this puts God squarely in control of each and every event that occurred in the Holocaust and all pandemics. What loving and good God would cause such suffering? What God who cared for humans and their well-being would have a divine will that ultimately "ordered" such severe excess and unlimited extremity?

Oord's second and third options, which partially overlap, assert that God guarantees human free will by granting us genuine choice *but* makes this "conditional," since from time to time God reserves the right to intervene when things have gone too bad or have ventured too far astray. From any reasonable point of view, did the Holocaust (or the bubonic plague or the Spanish flu or COVID-19) go too far? If God had the power to obviate or at least mitigate these events, why did God not do so?

While human freedom may go some distance in accounting for the Holocaust, if God had the power to curtail it, why did God not do so—especially if God is loving and good, and always wants what is best and most righteous for humans? And regarding diseases such as COVID-19 (which are termed as "natural evil"), human freedom does not create the disease (though humans irresponsibly and negligently can put themselves in situations or conditions which jeopardize health and well-being): Human choice (not to mask, not to socially distance, not to get the vaccines and boosters) *does* enter in; but humans did not choose the disease to exist in the first place.

In terms of Oord's fifth option, God as an impersonal Force, this removes God from interaction with the world and most importantly from a personal relationship with humans: Whether theologian Paul Tillich's "Ground of Being,"[13] "in whom we live and move and have our being" (Acts 17:28), or Einstein's notion of an "impersonal God" who created as First

---

13. Tillich, *Systematic Theology*, 235–39.

Cause but does not relate, these stand at odds with the biblical tradition of a God who "gets personal" with the world and "mixes it up" with the comings and goings of people's lives on earth. What has happened here to the belief in a God who cares deeply about human situations and struggles, human plights and perils, human joys and triumphs, and as a result is somehow "involved"? What does this perspective "do" to Christian doctrines such as the Incarnation (the Word of God becoming flesh in the person of Jesus born in Bethlehem) and divine providence (a God who "acts" in history and in nature to benefit God's people—such as in the exodus of Israelites from Egypt and the resurrection of Jesus on Easter morning)?

Though this option removes God from responsibility for evil and suffering (the Holocaust is the result of human sin, and pandemics are the result of natural laws), it has sacrificed the *agapé* love of God and the interrelationship between Creator and creation and the relationship of a personal God to persons "made in the divine image" (Gen 1:26-28).

Related to this is Oord's sixth option, in which God is seen as an "absentee Landlord," one who provided our "earth home" for and to us and now watches it from afar, from "out of the neighborhood." Here the transcendence of God has been preserved, however, at the loss of the immanence of God. God created the world, but God is not engaged in the creation. Here, also, God observed the Holocaust and witnessed the deaths largely of seniors from COVID-19 but did nothing to prevent it or curtail it.

Instead, God was the Primordial Originator of all things but is not a Current Actor amid or among them—in short, God is a Creator, not a Savior. From this perspective, God is acknowledged, so this view is theistic and unitarian, but it is not trinitarian: Jesus is a good human being who models the most meaningful way to live and who inspires us to do the same. Though we are not helped along this journey, we are simply shown the way. We are on our own.

Or, as another possibility, Jesus is like a "space invader," a sort of E.T. the extraterrestrial, who rocketed to earth from afar. He is not like us, but his memory nevertheless appeals to us as humans to accept him as Lord and Savior and dedicate our lives to being his followers and adopting his ethical way of life.

Also, the work of the Spirit is lost in this point of view: There is no regenerative Agent that can transform our lives and motivate or enable us to pursue the good life of the "fruits of the spirit" (Gal 5:22-23). Instead, and again, it's entirely and finally up to us; for there is no divine help in any form. Besides creating the world, what has God done for us? Reflecting Janet Jackson's hit pop song from nearly forty years ago, "What Have You Done for Me Lately?" the answer is nothing.

In addition, how could prayer be appropriate to this understanding of God's reality and God's power and love? How could prayer be functional in light of God's transcendence and non-engagement? According to the Christian tradition, the intention of prayer is to glorify and thank God for God's grace and goodness shown to the world and demonstrated in loving actions toward us; to share intimately and genuinely with God our triumphs and our troubles; to beseech God for God's forgiveness for our confessed shortcomings humbly and contritely shared; and to honestly petition God for divine action. But if God is not engaged with the world—since the location of God is far beyond our earthly domicile and God has nothing to do with our lives in the world—then what is the purpose of prayer in general and petitionary prayer in particular? Perhaps to ask for a miracle from afar, a divine intrusion into the causal nexus of things, a suspension of God's natural laws to benefit a human situation? If petitions are for divine intervention, besides for the possibility of breakings-in to life in the real world, then asking for God's action as a present Agent of change in the world would seem to provide mere psychological benefit at the very most and likely to constitute wasted breath.

In terms of Oord's seventh and final option, and as twentieth-century theologian Karl Barth would testify, God is transcendent, and therefore God is inexhaustible before our powers of examination and scrutiny. Who do we think we are? Reminiscent of God's reply to Job ("Who are we? Where were *we* when the Great Creator was causing everything to be that came to be?"), humility is warranted here. Human presumption to be able to fully discover and divulge God's will and to examine and completely understand God's actions is arrogant and filled with *hubris*. Barth goes so far as to insist that the otherness of God (God is both wholly Other and holy Other) is such that God is veiled, and even when God reveals God's self in revelation (through the Bible, supremely in and through Jesus, and through preaching and teaching in the church), what God reveals is that "God is veiled."[14]

Taking this even further, a fully "apophatic" theology (a theology that asserts that humans can know nothing at all about God) leaves humans floundering for knowledge about God and forced to hold "blind" or "nearly blind" faith. If/since faith may be understood as "trust," is there "enough"

---

14. Barth, *Church Dogmatics* 1.1:88; McCormack, *Orthodox and Modern*, 110.

here to warrant such trust? Faith may be defined biblically as "the assurance of things hoped for, the conviction of things not seen" (Heb 11:1), but is such faith or trust warranted when nothing at all is seen or known?

That leaves option four as the most attractive. However, this option diminishes the "vertical" power of God (its "omni-" degree) but does not eliminate God's power. For God's "horizontal" power is the power to influence, to persuade, to lure, to call, and to draw forth, and it is pervasive and persistent. Recall that Dr. Oord qualified this option in that he argued that God does not choose this limitation, as if God could have opted otherwise. Instead, that's the way God is.

Accordingly, God draws us to God's self—God's power is persuasive, not coercive. God is like a GPS, setting forth directions, but not requiring one to follow them. If that person does so, s/he arrives at the destination, which is the equivalent of God's will being "done on earth as it is in heaven." But if that person does not do so but goes another direction—which is errant and not in accord with God's will—then God will "recalculate" and send another direction which would get that person from the missed route back to the route God would prefer that s/he takes. In all instances, God is calling the individual forth with the proper way to go. However, it is up to that person to follow those directions. Again, when the individual does so, God's will is accomplished. When that person does not do so, God's will is temporarily frustrated. But because God loves human beings and cares for them, God does not give up on them: God continues to beckon them to the way that is God's will for them, what is best for them ("best" in the sense of what is "most good," which *can* entail what is *not* self-serving or preferential).

In this way of thinking about God, if a person goes the wrong way, God does not automatically correct him/her and jerk that person onto the path God knows is right for that individual. God does not control how s/he chooses to go. God does not determine the individual's direction in terms of making him/her go that way. God determines that person's direction in the sense of God presenting what is best for him/her—"best" meaning the healthiest, most faithful way to go and to be. It should be noted that the "best" for someone may sometimes involve self-sacrifice or suffering: Reaching out to the outcast or the ostracized may involve reactions from others that are not affirming or appreciative. Speaking truth to power could result in penalty or even death for the speaker. Jesus's sacrifice for the sake of others involved death. And Jesus wrestled with this in the Garden of

Gethsemane, just as we wrestle with God's leading and direction. But, regardless, it's up to the individual to decide. We have that freedom, and through our choices we exercise that freedom.

But does God not intervene to correct a person because God *chooses* not to do so—in effect, God could *make* us go the way God wants, but God stops short of this? No, God does not have absolute power in the sense that God *could* forcibly "make" the person go that direction by choosing that way. So, God must lament some humans' choices because God wishes they would have chosen otherwise; and then God comes back to them with the best possible way to go given what they have already chosen.

Here, God is more like a parent than a dictator—and a parent not like that of toddlers or teenagers but of mature adults: If a toddler chooses to step out in front of an approaching auto or touch a hot stove or place something poisonous into his/her mouth, a parent would intervene because the parent *could* intervene. The parent has the power and elects to enforce the healthiest situation for the child. If a teenager chooses to drink irresponsibly or to dabble in harmful drugs, the parent has the power and elects to intervene and help the young adult correct the behavior.

But if a parent is like the father or mother of a mature adult, he/she may not have the power to step in and redeem the situation or intervene to set things right. It's not that the parent would not wish to do so, it is the case that the parent *cannot* do so.

So, it is with God: Since God is not the divine parent of toddlers or teenagers, but of mature adults, God can give advice because God knows what is truly healthiest and is the "best" way for that person to go; God can constantly be involved through caring and suggesting because God's love is inclusive and inexhaustible. But God cannot *determine* the outcome. God's power expresses itself through enticement, not force, because that is what is possible for God. Total control is not feasible for God, even though God, at times (not to mention human parents), may wish that that were the case.

In terms of the Holocaust, this means that God did not *cause* the Holocaust: God did not impose suffering upon and kill six million Jewish people (and over four million gentiles, non-Jews, who were targeted as well) as punishment for their individual and collective sins. Nor did God send the Holocaust as a "test" to strengthen the spiritual backbone of those who remained faithful theists in spite of their horrible circumstances.

Nor did God *permit* what happened in the Holocaust to occur, as though God could have miraculously intervened and thwarted the Nazis' attempts at extermination and ended their Final Solution with a snap of divine fingers. While God *does* respect human freedom and free choice by following our decisions to their consequences and circumstances, God is constantly affirming our good decisions and responding to our bad ones, giving us options to realize what is possible in the particular, resultant situations. But God does not have the power to usurp those situations and rectify them unilaterally nor wave a magic wand to make everything all right again by dissolving the past.

So, God did not look on as an absentee landlord and survey the damage done but could have swooped in to make amends. Instead, God identified with both the victims and the victimizers, trying to persuade the latter to do otherwise and suffering with the former. To expect God to have come down or entered in with a thunderbolt of lightning to prevent the young boy from being hanged and having his body contorted for over half an hour before he died was impossible. That is not the way God's power is available and administered, because that is not the way God's power *is*.

Likewise, in terms of pandemics such as COVID-19, God did not *cause* these diseases: God did not wish to punish victims and the bereaved—not to mention those who were afflicted but survived after substantial anxiety and suffering—for their moral flaws and foibles. Nor did God send the pandemics as a "test" to determine who would remain faithful and theistic despite their pain and their loss of loved ones. Beyond this, since God is considered in traditional theology to be all-knowing (omniscient), God would already have been aware of the outcome; so, no test would have been necessary.

Nor did God *permit* what happened during the coronavirus, as though God could have miraculously intervened and thwarted the contraction of the disease and its spread. While God *does* respect human freedom and free choice (to mask or not to mask; to be vaccinated or not to be), God confirms our good decisions and responds to our bad ones by presenting us options to do what is then realizable in the aftermath of those personal mistakes. But God does not have the power to redo those situations and make everything fine again by eliminating the past.

And instead of observing from afar, God identified with both the victims and those who loved them. God truly wished that pandemics did not occur; and when they do, God's heart is genuinely wrenched, and God's compassion and love are specially evoked.

These situations of suffering caused by moral evil and natural causes point to a God whose power is less than omnipotent. But God is not anemic, for God's power is tremendous—not in a "vertical" or hierarchical sense of being sufficient to do whatever God wants and to cause to happen whatever God wishes would occur, but in a "horizontal" sense of influencing every living entity in God's creation. God cannot force things to happen, but God can entice things to happen. It's the way a Gardener facilitates the growth of a plant or flower—God nourishes it, but the living thing will grow the way its processes determine or "decide." God nourishes human beings, but human beings decide the way they will choose and how they will grow.

As noted previously, this notion of God as a Gardener is an image promoted by the late Ian Barbour (who was among the first persons, if not the first person, to advocate and write about the benefits and the challenges of a dialogue between religion and science).[15] Contemporary theologian Catherine Keller also suggests it.[16] The idea of God as a Gardener seems a helpful replacement for the more traditional idea of God as a King. A Gardener plants seeds but does not cause the plants to grow. He/she nourishes the growth but does not order it because he/she cannot do so. The power involved here is to help bring forth the product, not to directly produce the growth himself/herself.

A king, on the other hand, *rules* over his kingdom. His royal word is considered law, and his actions are believed to be irresistible. His control is therefore absolute, his commands firmly unquestionable (his word is embodied in the sword). He issues commands, and he administers by executive fiat. He determines how things will go and what shall be, and citizens of the realm are expected to kowtow and march in step. If not, his anger will be provoked, dissent will not be tolerated, democracy is not a prerogative, rebellions will be squashed, and oppositional leaders will be vanquished. He is in complete control.

Mathematician and philosopher Alfred North Whitehead noted that these kinds of kingly characteristics were applied early on to God. "The Church gave unto God the attributes which belonged exclusively to Caesar."[17] God's Word—the words (*dabarim*) of the Commandments (*mitzvot*)—was the religious (and political) law of the land. God thus "commanded" and ruled by heavenly fiat. He was in charge of how things

---

15. Barbour, *Religion in an Age of Science*, 76.
16. Keller, "Gallop of the Pale Green Horse," 50.
17. Whitehead, *Process and Reality*, 342.

went and what came to be. If the people—whether Israelites initially or Christians eventually—did not worship this God (and this God alone) and follow his rules, then his jealousy and wrath would be provoked, alternatives would not be tolerated, theocracy ruled out democracy, waywardness in sin would be severely punished (whether by military or natural catastrophe, such as exile and flooding, respectively, for instance) and leaders (even kings themselves, like Saul, for example) would be deposed.

Any notion of God as nurturer—God as Gardener—was concomitantly pruned. Scholars of Jewish history and biblical theology have long pointed out the faith journey of Israel and its need to distinguish that theology and faith journey from the Canaanite religion of the "land overflowing with milk and honey." For Canaanite religion was polytheistic, not monotheistic, and featured two key fertility deities, Baal, the god of the storm and the rain, and Ashtart (Asherah), the goddess of the soil and the earth. The "mating" of these deities was responsible for agricultural growth and abundant harvests. When the Israelites ceased being nomads after forty years in the wilderness following their liberation and departure from Egypt, they became settlers in the land of Canaan. No longer desert-dwellers, they became farmers, and their concern became more tending their farm rather than exclusively herding their sheep in the desert. Consequently, they flirted with Baal and Ashtart (Asherah). Some scholars have argued that the Israelites developed a practice of worshiping both the God of history and liberation *and* the gods of nature and fecundity.[18]

Biblical archaeologist William Dever is one who has cogently indicated this practice.[19] The warrior-God of the Exodus, involved in divine escape and divine partisanship in battle, was now associated with the nature-God of settling down and tending the fields. Eventually, the powerful God of the covenant in history would be combined with the awesome, procreative Power of nature. This combination is clear in the covenant-renewal ceremony in Neh 9. The priest Ezra (fifth century BCE), who brought one contingent of exiles back to Israel from their previous captivity in Babylon, offers a long prayer (found in verses 6–31). The prayer begins with an affirmation that God is the Creator:

> You have made heaven, the heaven of heavens, with all their host, the earth and all that is on it, the seas and all that is in them. (9:6)

---

18. Cross, *Canaanite Myth and Hebrew Epic*, 52–60.
19. Dever, *Does God Have a Wife?*; cf. Robert Wright, *Evolution of God*.

Then the prayer accents the call of Abraham (Abram) and the covenant God made with him as the father of the nation:

> You... chose Abram... and made with him the covenant to give to his offspring the land. (9:7–8)

Then the people's deliverance by God from Egypt is remembered:

> And you saw the affliction of our fathers in Egypt and heard their cry at the Red Sea, and performed signs and wonders against Pharaoh. (9:9–11)

Here the God of the Exodus—the Liberator God—is connected to the God of nature—the Creator God. There was no need to go after other gods to have both bases covered; God was not only the Lord of history, but also now the Lord of the harvest.

Prior to this covenant-renewal ceremony, the other ceremonies honored only the liberating God of the Exodus from Egypt. In Exod 19:3–8, the people must celebrate that it was God who brought the people out of bondage in the land of Egypt. Deuteronomy 11:7 is a reminder that God liberated the people, so they must respond by obeying God's commandments. In Deut 26:5–11, the people recall that God heard the cries of his afflicted people in Egypt and brought them out to a "land flowing with milk and honey." Joshua 24:1–13 proclaims that God "set free and liberated God's people." So now, in response, the people should "fear the Lord and serve Him." There is no mention of God being the Creator in these covenant-renewal ceremonies. But then, in Neh 9, God as Liberator and God as Creator are consolidated into one.

So, the delineation of the warrior God of the wilderness wanderers from the fertility gods of the predecessor peoples of the promised land gave way to a combination of the God of history and the God of nature into one deity. God was the Lord of both realms of human life. Be that as it may, there has been a lopsided emphasis since that time on the traditional imagery of God as warrior King rather than God as Gardener. But the notion of God as Tender of the Garden yields a better understanding of the way God's power works in the world and the way that God loves us.

It should be noted that this image God as Gardener is stereotypically feminine. While the stereotypical concept of God as King highlights power, with the human response of obedience and discipline (or else!), the concept of God as Tender of the Garden accents tenderness and gentleness, allowing and encouraging things to grow (with the human response of gratitude and cooperation). Here God is not demanding, but nurturing.

Julian of Norwich and Hildegard of Bingen, especially, felt very comfortable and theologically justified in addressing God as "She" and "Mother."[20] The maternal and the paternal, though stereotypical, were both preserved in one deity, not in multiple gods. As Hildegard put it,

> Through this fountain of life came the embrace of God's maternal love, which has nourished us unto life and is our help in perils, and is the deepest and sweetest charity and prepares us for penitence.[21]

Along these lines, theologian Thomas Oord has coined a word, "amipotence," to replace "omnipotence" as the priority characteristic of God's nature. "Divine love (*ami*) comes logically and conceptually prior to divine power (*potens*) . . . Love comes first."[22] Stereotypically, this is more "feminine" than "masculine," more like a "gardener" who nurtures than a "king" who exercises absolute rule.

This alternative concept of God, of divine power, and of divine love may seem difficult because traditionally, a number of persons (some? many? most?) have "pictured" God primarily or near exclusively as "male" and as all-powerful (and rather aloof and easily angered)—as able to do whatever God wants to do, whenever God chooses, and wherever God elects. From that perspective, for God to *be* God, that is what must be required. Unlimited power (omni-power; omnicausality) is the primary characteristic of God; divine love is not excluded but is subsumed under all-controlling divine dominance. While this admittedly provides psychological comfort (everything happens according to God's will, so there *must* have been a good, divine purpose in the bubonic plague and in the Spanish flu and in COVID-19 and in the Holocaust), it suffers from another angle a legitimate questioning of God's goodness and love. So, instead of providing comfort, it ultimately leads to discomfort.

If God *caused* such things as a pandemic or any sort of genocide, then what good and loving God would have been responsible for such tragedy and suffering? It could even suggest that God is not a good and beneficent deity, but an evil one, and not loving, but nasty. There *have* been moments in time and in cultures where God was portrayed as a "cosmic Sadist" who

---

20. Julian of Norwich, *Revelations of Divine Love*; Cain, *Attunement*, ch. 2.
21. Hildegard of Bingen, *Scivias*, II.2.4.
22. Oord, *Death of Omnipotence*, 120–21.

needed to be appeased through worship and through sacrifices, including those of humans. And there have been moments in time and in cultures where God has been portrayed not as a single deity but as multiple deities—some benevolent and some malevolent—who needed to be befriended or allied as a cohort or won over and appeased as an opponent.

But this all-powerful, everything-that-happens-does-so-according-to-divine-will concept of God places God as the Autocrat of the world, an all-controlling and uncontrollable Force by whose decrees and actions the happenings of the world occur. Thus, whatever happens—however heinous and devastating—has an ultimate, even mysterious meaning in the purposes and plans of God. And justice will be meted out, sooner or later, since perpetrators will eventually be held accountable, either in this world or ultimately in the next, and righteous sufferers will be rewarded, either on this earth or finally in heaven.

So, is a God any less powerful than this worthy of being called "God"? Doesn't God need to be this divine Dictator whose power is irresistible and whose ways are irrefutable? Is not God the *mysterium tremendum*[23]—the Mystery before whom one trembles—whose awesome power and transcendent majesty are greater than can be conceived, so enormous as to be incomprehensible? And must we choose to do what's good because we fear the judgment of this awful and "full of awe" God for our doing otherwise?

Isn't Reformer John Calvin correct when he asserted, "Nothing happens contrary to God's will, even that which is contrary to God's will?"[24] So, everything that happens occurs because it is God's will. And, as we have seen, that affirmation renders its concomitant God-concept unacceptable. In Archibald MacLeish's play *JB*, the suggestion is made, "If God is God, He is not good . . . If He is good, He is not God."[25] Scottish philosopher David Hume, in his *Dialogues Concerning Natural Religion*, quotes ancient philosopher Epicurus:

> Is God willing to prevent evil, but not able? Then he is impotent. Is he able, but not willing? Then He is malevolent. Is He both able and willing, then where does evil come from?[26]

---

23. Otto, *Idea of the Holy*.
24. Calvin, *Secret Providence of God*, 81.
25. MacLeish, *JB*, 11.
26. Hume, *Dialogues Concerning Natural Religion*, 66.

LOVE AS THE PRIMARY DIVINE CHARACTERISTIC

In order to avoid these pitfalls, it must be contended that God did not only not cause them, God also did not permit them. For seeing God through the filter of Jesus—envisioning God symbolically through Jesus's love—means that God neither produced nor allowed these events. In short, COVID-19 was contrary to God's will. In short, the Holocaust was contrary to God's will.

As a result, the traditional concept of God needs to change! It is "dead"; it no longer speaks to our experience of pandemics and holocausts. If what we understand as "God" is inadequate to address the enormity and gravity of pain and suffering, then we ought to change, in conversation with the biblical materials, with the best of rational thought, and with our experience, what we mean by "God."

A God who loves, and because of this, lures us toward what is good, what is true, what is healthy, and what is beautiful, is a God-concept that speaks to our existence in the world and our individual lives which experience hardship, heartache, pain, disappointment, pleasure, delight, and joy. And God's will is accomplished—when it *is* accomplished—by humans' partnership with God to actualize what God would prefer . . . and what we ultimately, ideally, know is best, is most righteous.

And since God's primary characteristic—God's "number one" attribute—is love, God attempts to affect us in loving ways, and God responds to us in loving ways. God is both "giver" and "receiver" in this process. That also means that God feels the pain of the world; God is not a detached observer who rules the kingdom from the distance of a throne in a palace on a celestial hill. Instead, God is in the midst of that pain, working from the inside to make a positive difference—*if* God's will (intentions, suggestions, influences) is obeyed and followed. As Alfred North Whitehead pointed out nearly one hundred years ago,

> I affirm that God does suffer as he participates in the ongoing life of the society of being. His sharing in the world's suffering is the supreme instance of knowing, accepting, and transforming in love the suffering which arises in the world. I am affirming the divine sensitivity. Without it, I can make no sense of the being of God.[27]

There is, then, a synergism or partnership between God and humans in realizing God's will for and in the world. God alone cannot do it, for God needs human decision-making and human action to accomplish that will.

---

27. Whitehead, "Suffering and Being," in *Adventures of Ideas*, 91–92.

As a result, God's power is bilateral—God's will needs God's power *and* the responsive power that people provide to partner with God to accomplish God's will, God's intention, God's preferences for the world. And without God's constant, unfailing, infinite love, the human element of that partnership would go uninformed, unmotivated, and undirected. In sum, we are needy, for we cannot do it alone; God is needy, for God cannot do it alone. We are not self-sufficient; God is not self-sufficient. The world needs God, but God also needs the world.[28]

This means that "we're God's hands and feet."[29] God inspires, and we choose either to respond positively or to reject God's direction. When we choose to follow God's lead, then God's will is accomplished (in that instant and in that instance). When we do not, then God's will is not. In all instances, God presents to us the "possibility" of what is best in light of the circumstances of the given situation. But it is our responsibility to join with God in the task of achieving God's intention (will) in that instance. If we comply and cooperate, then what God wants is accomplished. If we do not, then God's will is thwarted. Again, God is our divine Partner. Through this divine-human synergism, pain and suffering can be reduced.

The biblical witness in notable and key instances indicates this synergism between God and humans: God motivates Moses to lead a people out of bondage in Egypt. God calls Abraham to go to an unknown place. God works through David to gain success over an enemy (the Philistines) and its hero, Goliath. God does not unilaterally "cause" these things to happen but depends upon the cooperation of the specific humans. God persuades, and persons make their response. God does not (cannot) save the world alone. Together, we save the world.

> God's power is persuasive. God cannot make us do one thing or another. Rather, God influences, persuades, lures, or calls us to embrace the principles of God's vision in every context.[30]

This "fusion of activity"[31]—this cooperative process—results in God's will becoming successful in that situation.

Surely, it was God's will that we join with God in responding to the plague, the Spanish flu, and COVID-19. God did not cause these maladies

---

28. Cobb, *God and the World*.
29. Oord, *Death of Omnipotence*, 66; see also 141–76.
30. Coleman, *Making a Way*, 59.
31. The phrase is Tom Oord's in *Death of Omnipotence*, 20.

to occur; God did not permit them to assault us. But God was active in God's loving power trying to persuade us to respond by helping others. In fact, several scholars have noted the ways in which Christians helped others who were afflicted with disease or poverty or hunger. The church has always helped folks, they point out, and has been on the front lines and first responders throughout the history of plagues and pandemics. Church members have identified with the sick, the outcast, the poor, and the oppressed and cared for them. Indeed, the early church distinguished itself by reaching out to others to assist them in their distress. One scholar even argues that it was this ecclesiastical characteristic that was the primary reason for the growth of the Christian movement in its first few centuries.[32] Also, Bishop N. T. Wright points to the help provided by the church, both in ancient times and in the midst of the contemporary COVID-19 pandemic.[33]

The same has been the case with the Holocaust. Though God neither caused nor permitted that attempted genocide, God worked to get people to help those who had been discredited, disenfranchised, targeted, persecuted, deported, and destined for murder. Not enough persons responded to thwart completely the Nazis' actions; but a number *did* react and help. Accounts of their courage, their struggle, their sacrifice, and their success have been disseminated today, and more are being currently researched and circulated.[34]

When persons wrestle with what to do and choose to do that which God wants and that to which God is luring or persuading them, then God's will is accomplished in that moment and for that time. Humans need God in this process, for God's loving power can motivate us to do the thing, to undertake the action, that conforms to God's intention in that situation. And God needs humans in order for God's will to be fulfilled. Rabbi Richard Rubenstein liked to say that "God is the ocean, we are the waves."[35]

---

32. Stark, *Rise of Christianity*, ch. 4: "Epidemics, Networks, and Conversion."

33. N. T. Wright, *God and the Pandemic*, 2–4.

34. Of course, the names of Raoul Wallberg, Oskar Schindler, Chiune Sugihara, Miep Gies, the French town of LeChambon-sur-Lignon, and Maximilian Kolbe are well known examples in this regard. Examples of new names added to the list include Irena Sendler, Tina Strobos, the Dutch town of Nieuwlande, Dimitar Peshev, the Assisi Network, Ho Feng-Shan, Carl Lutz, King Boris III, and Bulgarian Archbishops Stefan and Kyril.

35. Berger, "Richard Rubenstein, 97, Dies"; Rubenstein "undermine[s] traditional conceptions of an all-powerful God who manipulates human behavior like a puppeteer wielding marionettes."

Helpful here is the notion in the Jewish tradition of the two *yetzers*: One *yetzer* ("spirit" or "inclination") is attracting us to do what is good, what is right, what is best in a given situation; the other *yetzer* ("spirit" or "inclination") is tempting us to succumb to doing what is the opposite of this, that which is unhealthy, perhaps selfish or egotistical, that which goes against God's suggestion for God's will to be actualized.

When we pursue trying to do the good because that is what is "best" (i.e., most righteous) for us, what is good and healthy and loving, we trust that God is "speaking" to us and drawing us in that direction. But it is not *guaranteed* that we will journey toward the good, the healthy, and the loving. There is a chance we will "sin"—in effect, do that which is wrong for us, unhealthy, bad, evil, unloving.

Thus, in summary, there are two spirits (*yetzers*) inside us which vie for our attention and our loyalty and our actualization. One spirit implores and entices us to do good; one spirit tempts us and inveigles us to do bad. So, every day is a wrestling match. In fact, the word "Israel" means "[the one who] wrestles with God."

A Christian example of this Jewish sense of "wrestling" is the story of Father Makarios. Father Makarios lived on top of the jagged peak mountains in Greece along with the other monks who share time and space in the monastery of Mount Athos. One day when he descended in one of those baskets that are let down and drawn up to go shopping in the market, one of the villagers asked, "Father Makarios, what are you doing up there on top of the mountain?" Makarios answered, "We are wrestling with God!" The villager continued, "So, do you hope to win, Father?" Makarios replied, "Oh no, my friend, we hope to lose."[36]

Surrendering to God's will—losing the wrestling match—is the intention and objective of persons of faith. We are to surrender our will to the divine will, we are to give up our own selfish wants and give in to the leading of God. As Jesus, the model of our faith, prayed in the Garden of Gethsemane, "Not my will, but yours be done, O God" (Matt 26:39b; Mark 14:36; Luke 22:42; cf. John 5:30b). Sometimes, persons of faith are successful in this; sometimes they are not.

From the Muslim perspective, Jesus here shows himself to be a "muslim," because in that tradition, surrendering one's will to the will of God categorizes one as a "muslim." The Arabic word "Islam" means the "peace that comes when one surrenders his/her will to God's will" or, in short,

---

36. Rolheiser, *Domestic Monastery*, 69.

"submission to God." And *jihad*—often mistranslated as "holy war"—refers primarily to the inner struggle in a person between doing right and doing wrong, and only secondarily to a defensive war to ensure one's religious freedom. This is similar to the two *yetzers* in Judaism and the Father Makarios story from Mount Athos in Greece.

In this process of God's persuasive power and luring love and human obedient or disobedient response, both humans and God are affected. God impacts us humans, and we humans impact God. At every instance of existence, God is calling us to do the right thing, the best thing, the thing that is in accord with God's will. And we choose either to follow that call, that leading, or to go a different direction. If we choose another way, because God loves us, God does not give up on us; God then comes to us again with another persuasion, another call, another lure. God's will is contingent upon human response and influenced by that response. And human response is influenced by God's participation in our decision-making.

This means that God not only influences the world, but also the world influences God.[37] The world not only needs God, but God also needs the world. God truly matters to humans, and humans really matter to God. God loves humans, and humans are capable of loving God. God feels the pain and suffering in and from the world; and the world can feel God in the midst of that pain and suffering, working from the inside to make a positive difference—*if* God's will (intentions, suggestions, influences) is obeyed and followed.

God is actually and inevitably affected by what happens in the world—by distresses as well as delights, failures as well as successes, defeats as well as victories, moral travesties as well as moral triumphs, diseases as well as health. However, this stands in contrast to what Christian theology has traditionally and regularly affirmed: The doctrine of the "impassibility of God" contends that, since God is sufficient alone, God is unaffected by world happenings and human decisions and actions.

Clement of Alexandria (second century CE) asserted that God has no emotions or passions. "God is impassible, free of anger, destitute of desire."[38] Clement was not a solo voice here, for a chorus of other second-century Church Father theologians voiced the same point of view—Ignatius

---

37. Cobb, *God and the World*.

38. Clement of Alexandria, *Stromata* IV, xxiii, in Roberts and Donaldson, *Ante-Nicene Fathers*, 2:437.

of Antioch,[39] Justin Martyr,[40] and Irenaeus,[41] among them. In addition, Augustine of Hippo, writing early in the fifth century, followed suit: "God is first and foremost characterized by immutability" (since emotions evidenced a change, and because God could not change, therefore God was immutable and impassible).[42] Speaking to this issue in the eleventh century, Anselm realized the tension between impassibility and the picture and actions of God in the Bible. He resolved this imbroglio by claiming that though God in God's self was impassible, God *seems* to be passible from a human angle of vision: "Thou art compassionate [passible] in terms of our experience, and not compassionate [impassible] in terms of Thy being."[43] Finally, in the thirteenth century, Thomas Aquinas used the following syllogism to "solve" the dilemma: "For in God there are no passions. Now love is a passion, Therefore, love is not in God." Realizing the inadmissibility of this conclusion, Thomas made a distinction between two elements within love, one which is passionate and one which is not. He went on to say, then, that God "loves without passion."[44]

But how can an impassible God (i.e., a God unaffected by happenings in the world) identify with the joys and sorrows of creatures in the world? How can God love in a way identifiable with the human experience of love? Human love, as we know it, means giving and receiving, affecting and being affected. And since human love is an analogy or symbol for God's love (otherwise, to say that "God is love" carries no meaning at all!), can God truly love if God is not affected? If God's love is not responsive, then is it fully and really love?

This has implications also for prayer. The purpose of prayer is to establish and maintain "rapport" with God.[45] Thus, prayer assumes having an impact on God. Humans pray, and this action has presumed more than just words directed into space and/or psychological peace of mind. Prayer is precipitated by the theological proclamation that prayer impacts God and

---

39. Ignatius of Antioch, *Epistle to Polycarp*, III.2, 46.

40. Justin Martyr, *First Apology*, XXV, in Roberts and Donaldson, *Ante-Nicene Fathers*, 1:171.

41. Irenaeus, *Against Heresies*, II.xvii.6, in Roberts and Donaldson, *Ante-Nicene Fathers*, 1:381–82.

42. Augustine of Hippo, *On the Trinity*, quoted in Sontag, *Divine Perfection*, 37.

43. Anselm of Canterbury, *Cur Deus Homo*, 13.

44. Aquinas, *Summa Theologica*, Q. 20, art. 1, obj. 1, and ans. 1.

45. Cain, *Rapport*, 11–13.

has a bearing on the comings and goings in the world. Religious people believe that prayer *means* something and *does* something! If God is unresponsive by God's very nature (*cannot* be responsive), then a basic foundation for the exercise and purpose of prayer has crumbled.

Theologians Kazō Kitamori and Jürgen Moltmann have underscored the notion of a God of *pathos*, a passible God, a God who is responsive as well as influential in the world (affected by, as well as affecting, the world). The former's *Theology of the Pain of God*[46] and the latter's *The Crucified God*[47] both point to the cross as a revelation that God suffers, is touched by human trauma and triumph, and is impacted by all that goes on in the world.

Theologian Edward Farley has also addressed this issue in his award-winning book, *Divine Empathy: A Theology of God*.[48] In what he terms "efficacious empathy," he describes God's empathy as itself a suffering, a suffering love. God is empathetically efficacious, and this constitutes God's activity in the world. God gives; God receives. God affects; God is affected.

Human love and genuine empathy mean identifying with " the other" and experiencing what he or she is experiencing; they involve providing and receiving. And since human love and human empathy are an analogy for God's love and God's empathy, can God truly love if God is not affected? If God's love is not responsive, then is it fully and really love? And can empathy be true empathy unless God feels our pain and is affected by the horror and agony we experience (as well as our joys and delights)?

As a result of these theologians' efforts, in view of God's empathic relationship to human pain and suffering, and in light of genuine love as the primary divine characteristic, "impassibility is a divine impossibility."[49]

The fourteenth-century bubonic plague ended the lives of twenty-five to fifty million people, over one-half the population of Europe. The early twentieth-century Spanish flu was contracted by one-third of the world's population and led to the deaths of fifty million persons; sixty-five thousand people died in the United States. COVID-19 caused the deaths of almost seven million persons worldwide and infected over one hundred million US citizens, resulting in over one million American deaths. Six million Jews were systematically murdered in the Nazi Holocaust. Five million others also viewed to be *Untermenschen* ("subhumans") were killed.

---

46. Kitamori, *Theology of the Pain of God*.
47. Moltmann, *Crucified God*.
48. Farley, *Divine Empathy*, especially 303–13.
49. Cain, "Passionate God?," 52–57.

A loving God did not "plan" these deaths. The suffering of the victims who died, and those who were brutalized or infected but lived, was *not* caused by God as a punishment or to teach sinful humans a "lesson." God did not "permit" these events in order to guarantee humans their freedom of choice and then choose not to intervene to prevent or to mitigate pain and suffering and death. Surely these maladies would have justified such intervention if God had had the necessary power to do so. Surely these tragedies did not serve any divine purpose or hinge on a cosmic reason for their occurrence.

Instead, a God who loves, who is intimately involved in persuading humans and the rest of creation, would not "will" them or "allow" them. God suffered with all those affected by these catastrophes, and then worked ceaselessly to draw the "best," the "good," from them ("In all things God works for good"—Rom 8:28). That's what it means to love; and God's chief characteristic is love.

Bibliography

Aberth, John. *The Black Death: The Great Mortality of 1348–1350*. New York: St. Martin's, 2005.
———. *From the Brink of the Apocalypse*. London: Routledge, 2009.
Almond, Philip C. *God: A New Biography*. London: Bloomsbury, 2018.
Al-Wardi, Ibn. "An Essay on the Report of the Pestilence." Translated by Michael W. Dols. In *Near Eastern Numismatics, Iconography, Epigraphy, and History*, edited by Dickran Kouymyjian, 447–54. Beirut: The American University of Beirut, 1974.
Anderson, Bernhard W. *Understanding the Old Testament*. 4th ed. Englewood Cliffs, NJ: Prentice-Hall, 1986.
Anselm of Canterbury. *Cur Deus Homo, Saint Anselm: Basic Writings*. Translated by Sidney N. Deane. La Salle, IL: Open Court, 1974.
Aquinas, Thomas. *Summa Theologica*. Vol. 1. Chicago: Encyclopedia Britannica, 1952.
Armstrong, Dorsey. *The Black Death: The World's Most Devastating Plague*. Chantilly, VA: The Teaching Company, 2016.
Armstrong, Karen. *A History of God*. New York: Knopf, 1993.
Aslan, Reza. *God: A Human History*. New York: Random House, 2017.
Augustine of Hippo. *City of God*. Cambridge, MA: Harvard University Press, 1957.
———. *On the Trinity: Basic Writings of St. Augustine*. Vol. 2. New York: Random House, 1948.
Austriaco, Nicanor. "For Christian Believers, What Does This Pandemic Mean?" *Providence College Bulletin* (Apr. 9, 2020).
Barbour, Ian. *Religion in an Age of Science*. New York: HarperCollins, 1990.
Barker, Sheila. "The Making of a Plague Saint: Saint Sebastian's Imagery and Cult Before the Counter-Reformation." In *Piety and Plague*, edited by Franco Mormando and Thomas Worcester, 90–127. Kirksville, MO: Truman University Press, 2007.
Barry, John. *The Great Influenza*. New York: Penguin, 2018.

BIBLIOGRAPHY

Barth, Karl. *Church Dogmatics*. Translated by Geoffrey W. Bromiley. Edinburgh: T & T Clark, 1975.
BBC. "Pandemic: The Story of the 1918 Flu." *The Documentary*, aired January 13, 2018.
Benton, Robert, dir. *Feast of Love*. MGM Studios, 2007. Streaming.
Berger, Joseph. "Richard Rubenstein, 97, Dies; Theologian Challenged Ideas of God." *New York Times*, June 9, 2021.
Bertherat, Eric, et al. "Plague Reappearance in Algeria After 50 Years." *Emerging Infectious Diseases* 13.10 (2007) 1459–62. DOI: 10.3201/eid1310.070284.
Blakemore, Erin. "Why Thomas Jefferson Rewrote the Bible Without Jesus' Miracles and Resurrection." *History*, Oct. 4, 2023. www.history.com/news/thomas-jefferson-bible-religious-beliefs.
Boccaccio, Giovanni. *The Decameron*. Toronto: McClelland and Stewart, 2020.
Bonhoeffer, Dietrich. *Letters and Papers from Prison*. Edited by Eberhard Bethge. Translated by Reginald Fuller. New York: Macmillan, 1972.
Boyce, Matthew, and Rebecca Katz. "The 1918 Influenza Pandemic and COVID-19." PBS, *American Experience*, Mar. 18, 2020. http://www.pbs.org/wgbh/americanexperience/features/1918-influenza-pandemic-and-covid-19/.
Breitzer, Susan. "American Religion and the Pandemic of 1918." Interview with Christopher Brick and Kariann Yokota, *Intervals* podcast, June 23, 2021. rebrand.ly/vchm8c2.
Browne, Janet. *Charles Darwin: A Biography*. Vol. 1. New York: Knopf, 1995.
Brueggemann, Walter. *Virus as a Summons to Faith: Biblical Reflections in a Time of Loss, Grief, and Anxiety*. Eugene, OR: Cascade, 2020.
Bryner, Jeanna. "First Known Case of Coronavirus Traced Back to November in China." Live Science, Mar. 14, 2020. https://www.livescience.com/first-case-coronavirus-found.html.
Cain, Clifford Chalmers. *Attunement: Living in Harmony with Nature*. Eugene, OR: Wipf & Stock, 2019.
———. "A Passionate God?" *St. Luke's Journal of Theology* 25.1 (1981) 52–57.
———. *Rapport: Praying to God*. Kearney, NE: Morris, 2017.
Calvin, John. *The Secret Providence of God*. Edited by Paul Helm. Wheaton, IL: Crossway, 2010.
Campbell, Olivia. "Medieval Pilgrims Apparently Tried to Ward Off the Plague with Bawdy Badges." *Atlas Obscura*, Jan. 29, 2021. https://www.atlasobscura.com/articles/medieval-plague-badges.
Camus, Albert. *The Plague*. New York: Knopf Doubleday, 1991.
Caplan, Jeremy. "Q and A: Rabbi Harold Kushner." *Time*, Oct. 12, 2006. https://time.com/archive/6908029/q-a-rabbi-harold-kushner/.
Case-Winters, Anna. *God's Power: Traditional Understandings and Contemporary Challenges*. Louisville: Westminster John Knox, 1990.
Catherine of Siena. *The Letters of Catherine of Siena*. Vol. 1. Translated by Suzanne Noffke. Tempe, AZ: Arizona Center for Medieval and Renaissance Studies, 2000.
Centers for Disease Control and Prevention. "CDC Museum COVID-19 Timeline." Last reviewed March 15, 2023. https://www.cdc.gov/museum/timeline/covid19.html.
———. "New COVID-19 Variants." Feb. 11, 2020.
Chaucer, Geoffrey. *The Canterbury Tales*. Edited by Nevill Coghill. London: Penguin, 1977.
China CDC Weekly. "The Epidemiological Characteristics of an Outbreak of 2019 Novel Coronavirus Diseases." 2.8 (2020) 113–22. DOI: 10.46234/ccdcw2020.032.

Christianity Today. "John Newton: Did You Know?" Jan. 2004. https://www.christianitytoday.com/2004/01/john-newton-did-you-know/.

Click, Julia. "Elie Wiesel's Unique Journey to Redemption." Undergraduate thesis, Bellarmine University, Louisville, Kentucky, 2017. https://scholarworks.bellarmine.edu/ugrad_theses/23.

Cobb, John B., Jr. *God and the World.* Eugene, OR: Wipf & Stock, 1969.

Cobb, John B., Jr., and David Ray Griffin. *Process Theology: An Introductory Exposition*: Philadelphia: Westminster, 1976.

Cohn, Norman. *The Pursuit of the Millennium.* Rev. ed. Oxford: Oxford University Press, 2007.

Cohn, Samuel, Jr. "The Black Death and the Burning of Jews." *Past and Present* 196.1 (2007) 3–36.

Coleman, Monica A. *Making a Way Out of No Way.* Minneapolis: Fortress, 2008.

Conrad, Lawrence I. "The Plague in the Early Medieval Near East." PhD diss., Princeton University, 1981.

Crosby, Alfred W. *America's Forgotten Pandemic.* Cambridge, UK: Cambridge University Press, 1989.

Cross, Frank. *Canaanite Myth and Hebrew Epic.* Cambridge, MA: Harvard University Press, 1973.

Curry, James R. *Children of God, Children of Earth.* Bloomington, IN: AuthorHouse, 2008.

Darwin, Charles. *The Autobiography of Charles Darwin.* Edited by Nora Barlow. New York: Norton, 1993.

Darwin, Francis, ed. *The Foundations of the Origin of Species.* Cambridge, UK: Cambridge University Press, 1909.

Defoe, Daniel. *A Journal of the Plague Year.* London, 1886. Project Gutenberg, 2023.

De' Mussi, Gabriele. *Historia de Morbo.* Translated by Rosemary Horrox. Manchester: Manchester University Press, 1994.

Desmon, Adrian, and James Moore. *Darwin: The Life of a Tormented Evolutionist.* New York: Warner, 1991.

DesOrmeaux, Anna Louise. "The Black Death and Its Effect on 14th and 15th Century Art." MA thesis, Louisiana State University, 2007.

Dever, William. *Does God Have a Wife? Archaeology and Folk Religion in Ancient Israel.* Grand Rapids: Eerdmans, 2005.

Doidge, Norman. "Plague as Punishment." *Tablet Magazine,* July 29, 2020. https://www.tabletmag.com/sections/science/articles/plague-as-punishment.

Dols, Michael W. "Plague in Early Islamic History." *Journal of the American Oriental Society* 94.3 (July–Sept. 1974) 371–88.

Doubleday, Simon. *After the Plague.* Chantilly, VA: The Teaching Company, 2022.

Duchemin, Pierre-André. "Bonhoeffer's Concept of the Weakness of God and Religionless Christianity in a World Come of Age." MA thesis, McGill University, 2009.

Dyer, Wayne W. *Your Erroneous Zones.* New York: Avon, 1976.

Editors of *Encyclopaedia Britannica.* "Sunda Strait." *Encyclopaedia Britannica,* last updated April 16, 2009. https://www.britannica.com/place/Sunda-Strait.

Ehrman, Bart. "First Lecture at Coral Gables Congregational Church." *The Bart Ehrman Blog,* Jan. 19, 2006. ehrmanblog.org/how-Jesus-Became-god-ucc-part-1-of-3.

Farley, Edward. *Divine Empathy: A Theology of God.* Minneapolis: Fortress/Augsburg, 1996.

Foa, Anna. *The Jews of Europe After the Black Death*. Oakland: University of California Press, 2000.

Frank, Anne. *The Diary of a Young Girl: The Definitive Edition*. Edited by Mirjam Pressler. New York: Bantam, 2021.

Gehrz, Chris. "What the 1918 Influenza Pandemic Meant for American Churches." *Anxious Bench*, Mar. 10, 2020. www.patheos.com/blogs/anxiousbench/2020/03/influenza-pandemic-1918-churches/.

Gill, Victoria. "Covid Origin Studies Say Evidence Points to Wuhan Market." BBC, July 26, 2022.

Gostin, Lawrence O., and Gigi K. Gronvall. "The Origins of COVID-19—Why It Matters (And Why It Doesn't)." *New England Journal of Medicine* 388 (June 22, 2023) 2305–8. www.nejm.org/doi/full/10.1056/NEJMp2305081.

Gottfried, Robert S. *The Black Death: Natural and Human Disaster in Medieval Europe*. London: Macmillan, 1983.

Greshko, Michael, and National Geographic Staff. "What Are Mass Extinctions, and What Causes Them?" *National Geographic*, Sept. 26, 2019. https://www.nationalgeographic.com/science/article/mass-extinction.

Griffin, David Ray. *God, Power, and Evil*. Louisville: Westminster John Knox, 2004.

Hao, Ying-Jian, et al. "The Origins of COVID-19 Pandemic: A Brief Overview." *Transbound and Emerging Diseases* (Oct. 20, 2022). DOI: 10.1111/tbed.14732.

Hart, David Bentley. *The Doors of the Sea: Where Was God in the Tsunami?* Grand Rapids: Eerdmans, 2011.

Hartshorne, Charles. *Omnipotence and Other Theological Mistakes*. Albany: SUNY Press, 1984.

Heymann, David L., and Nahoko Shindo. "Covid-19: What Is Next for Public Health?" *Lancet* 395.10224 (Feb. 22, 2020) 542–45.

Hildegard of Bingen. *Scivias [Know the Ways]*. Translated by Columba Hart and Jane Bishop. Mahwah, NJ: Paulist, 1990.

Hoag, Hannah. "Study Revives Bird Origin for 1918 Flu Pandemic." *Nature* (Feb. 16, 2014). doi.org/10.1038/nature.2014.14723.

Hochman, David. "Three Years In: How the Pandemic Has Changed Our Lives (And How It Hasn't)." *AARP Bulletin*, Mar. 7, 2023.

Horn, Trent. "Is COVID-19 a Punishment from God?" *Catholic Answers*, Mar. 24, 2020. www.catholic.com/magazine/online-edition/is-covid-19-a-punishment-from-God.

Horrox, Rosemary, ed. *The Black Death*. Manchester: Manchester University Press, 1994.

Huang, Chaolin, et al. "Clinical Features of Patients Infected with 2019 Novel Coronavirus in Wuhan, China." *The Lancet* 395.10223 (Jan. 30, 2020) 497–506.

Hume, David. *Dialogues Concerning Natural Religion*. New York: Hafner, 1948.

Ignatius of Antioch. *Epistle to Polycarp. An English Translation of the Epistles of St. Ignatius*. London: SPCK, 1934.

The Information Architects of *Encyclopaedia Britannica*. "Indian Ocean Tsunami of 2004: Facts and Related Content." *Encyclopaedia Britannica*, accessed Dec. 13, 2024. https://www.britannica.com/facts/Indian-Ocean-tsunami-of-2004.

Jiang, Xiaowei, and Ruoqi Wang. "Wildlife Trade Is Likely the Source of SARS-CoV-2." *Science* 377.6609 (Aug. 25, 2022) 925–26.

BIBLIOGRAPHY

Johnson, Ben. "The Great Flood and Great Famine of 1314." *Historic UK*, Mar. 24, 2015. https://www.historic-uk.com/HistoryUK/HistoryofEngland/The-Great-Flood-Great-Famine-of-1314/.

Johnson, Paul. Review of *God: A Biography*, by Jack Miles. *Commentary*, July 1995. https://www.commentary.org/articles/paul-johnson-3/god-a-biography-by-jack-miles/.

Julian of Norwich. *Revelations of Divine Love*. Garden City, NY: Image, 1977.

Kaifes, Frank. "'The Book of Job: When Bad Things Happened to a Good Person' by Harold S. Kushner." *Whosoever* (blog), May 1, 2013. https://whosoever.org/moral-god-and-immoral-nature-an-evening-with-rabbi-kushner/.

Kee, Caroline. "What to Know About Eris." *Today*, Aug. 16, 2023.

Keller, Catherine. "The Gallop of the Pale Green Horse." In *Pandemic, Ecology, and Theology: Perspectives on COVID-19*, edited by Alexander J. B. Hampton. London: Routledge, 2021.

Kessler, G. "Trump's False Claim That the WHO Said the Coronavirus Was 'Not Communicable.'" *Washington Post*, Apr. 17, 2020.

Kitamori, Kazō. *Theology of the Pain of God*. Richmond: John Knox, 1965.

Kohn, George C. *Encyclopedia of Plague and Pestilence*. New York: Checkmark Books, 2002.

Kokkinidis, Tasos. "Apollo vs. Agamemnon: The Plague in Ancient Greece Was Divine Wrath." *Greek Reporter*, Feb. 21, 2021. https://greekreporter.com/2021/02/21/apollo-vs-agamemnon-the-plague-in-ancient-greece-was-divine-wrath/.

Kolata, Gina. *The Story of the Great Influenza Pandemic of 1918 and the Search for the Virus That Caused It*. New York: Farrar, Straus and Giroux, 1999.

Kreis, Stephen. "Satan Triumphant: The Black Death." *The History Guide: Lectures on Ancient and Medieval European History*, July 2, 2014. Lecture 29.

Krijger, Tom-Eric. "Coping with COVID-19 in Dutch Christianity: A Comparison with the 1918 Spanish Flu Pandemic." *The Religion Factor* (blog), Apr. 24, 2020.

Kushner, Harold. *The Book of Job: When Bad Things Happened to a Good Person*. New York: Schocken, 2012.

———. *When Bad Things Happen to Good People*. New York: Schocken, 1981.

Lactantius. "On the Anger of God." https://epicurus.net/en/anger.html.

Laërtius, Diogenes. *Lives of the Eminent Philosophers*. Oxford: Oxford University Press, 2018.

Langland, William. *Piers Plowman: The C Version*. Translated by George Economou. Philadelphia: University of Pennsylvania Press, 1996.

LeMoult, John E. "Thou Shalt Not Let Hitler Win." *Dayton Daily News*, July 13, 2016. https://www.daytondailynews.com/news/opinion/thou-shalt-not-let-hitler-win/TDgTMbx8HKJqM4oYqDNZ4K/.

Levi, Primo. *Survival in Auschwitz*. Miami: Orion, 1959.

Lewis, C. S. *A Grief Observed*. London: Faber and Faber, 1961.

Li, Qun, et al. "Early Transmission Dynamics in Wuhan, China, of Novel Coronavirus-Infected Pneumonia." *New England Journal of Medicine* 382.13 (2020) 1199–207.

Linder, F. E., and R. D. Grove. *Vital Statistics Rates in the U.S.: 1900–1940*. Washington, DC: U.S. Government Printing Office, 1943.

Llanes, Hector. "Theology Thursday: God's Providence." Grand Canyon University (blog), Nov. 7, 2019. https://www.gcu.edu/blog/theology-ministry/theology-thursday-gods-providence.

Lucas, Henry S. "The Great European Famine of 1315, 1316, and 1317." *Speculum: A Journal of Mediaeval Studies* 5.4 (1930) 343–77.

MacKim, LindaJo H. "Amazing Grace." In *The Presbyterian Hymnal Companion*. Louisville: Westminster John Knox, 1993.

MacLeish, Archibald. *JB*. Boston: Houghton-Mifflin, 1961.

Malawani, Mukhamad, et al. "The 1257 CE Cataclysmic Eruption of Samalas Volcano." *Journal of Volcanology and Geothermal Research* 432 (2022) 6–7.

Mangrum, Todd. "The Pandemic as God's Judgment." *Christianity Today*, May 15, 2020.

Mark, Joshua J. "Medieval Cures for the Black Death." *World History Encyclopedia*, Apr. 15, 2020. https://www.worldhistory.org/article/1540/medieval-cures-for-the-black-death/.

———. "Religious Responses to the Black Death." *World History Encyclopedia*, Apr. 16, 2020.

Marshall, L. J. *Waiting on the Will of the Lord: The Imagery of the Plague*. Philadelphia: University of Pennsylvania, 1989.

Mathieu, Edouard, et al. "COVID-19 Pandemic." Our World in Data. https://ourworldindata.org/coronavirus.

McCormack, Bruce L. *Orthodox and Modern: Studies in the Theology of Karl Barth*. Grand Rapids: Baker, 2008.

McDaniel, Jay B. *Of God and Pelicans*. Louisville: Westminster John Knox, 1989.

———. *What Is Process Thought?* Claremont, CA: Process and Faith, 2008.

McHugh, Jess. "How the 1918 Pandemic Changed America, from Women's Rights to Germaphobia." *Washington Post*, Nov. 13, 2022.

Meier, Mischa. "The Justinianic Plague: The Economic Consequences of the Pandemic in the Eastern Roman Empire and Its Cultural and Religious Effects." *Early Medieval Europe* 24.3 (2016) 267–92.

Migliore, Daniel. *Faith Seeking Understanding*. 2nd ed. Grand Rapids: Eerdmans, 2004.

———. *The Power of God and the gods of Power*. Louisville: Westminster John Knox, 2008.

Miles, Jack. *God: A Biography*. New York: Knopf, 1995.

Moltmann, Jürgen. *The Crucified God*. London: SCM, 1974.

Mougel, Nadège. "World War I Casualties." Course Hero, 2011. Translated by Julie Gratz. https://www.coursehero.com/file/124077112/reperes112018pdf/.

Münchow, Thiess. "'God Is the Beyond in the Midst of Our Lives' (Dietrich Bonhoeffer): Considering Absentheism." *Disputatio Philosophia* (2015) 43–52. https://hrcak.srce.hr/file/222847.

News Wires. "China Confirms Sharp Rise in Cases of SARS-Like Virus Across the Country." France 24, Jan. 20, 2020. https://www.france24.com/en/20200120-china-confirms-sharp-rise-in-cases-of-sars-like-virus-across-the-country.

Nietzsche, Friedrich. *The Gay Science*. Translated by Josefine Nauckoff, edited by Bernard Williams. Cambridge, UK: Cambridge University Press, 2001.

———. *Thus Spoke Zarathustra: A Book for Everyone and No One*. London: Penguin, 1961.

Nirenberg, David. "Communities of Violence: Persecution of Minorities in the Middle Ages." In *The Black Death*, edited by Elizabeth A. Lehfeldt. New York: St. Martin's, 2004.

Nohl, Johannes. *The Black Death: A Chronicle of the Plague*. Yardley: Westholme, 2006.

Northwestern Medicine. "COVID-19 Pandemic Timeline." Updated March 2023. https://www.nm.org/healthbeat/medical-advances/new-therapies-and-drug-trials/covid-19-pandemic-timeline.

Nutton, Vivian. "Galen: Biography." *Encyclopedia Britannica*. Last updated October 10, 2024. https://www.britannica.com/biography/Galen.

O'Keefe, Tim. "Epicurus." *Internet Encyclopedia of Philosophy*, n.d. https://iep.utm.edu/epicur/.

O'Malley, Timothy. "Saints of the Black Death." *Church Life Journal*, Nov. 22, 2021. https://churchlifejournal.nd.edu/articles/saints-of-the-black-death/.

Oord, Thomas Jay. *The Death of Omnipotence and Birth of Amipotence*. Grasmere, ID: SacraSage, 2023.

———. *God Can't*. Grasmere, ID: SacraSage, 2019.

———. "Models of God's Action." *Thomas Jay Oord* (blog), Mar. 1, 2020. thomasjayoord.com/index.php/blog/archives/models-of-gods-action.

———. *The Uncontrolling Love of God*. Grand Rapids: InterVarsity, 2015.

Otto, Rudolf. *The Idea of the Holy*. 2nd ed. Oxford: Oxford University Press, 1958.

Paley, William. *Natural Theology, Or, Evidences of the Existence and Attributes of the Deity*. New York: E. Sargeant, 1802.

PBS. "The First Wave." *American Experience*, n.d. www.pbs.org/wgbh/americanexperience/features/influenza-first-wave/.

———. "Placing Blame." *American Experience*, n.d. www.pbs.org/wgbh/americanexperience/features/influenza-placing-blame/.

Pekar, Jonathan. "The Molecular Epidemiology of Multiple Zoonotic Origins of SARS-CoV-2." *Science* 377.6609 (Aug. 2022) 960–66.

Pellowe, John. "How the Church Responded to Previous Pandemics." Canadian Centre for Christian Charities, Jan. 11, 2021. http://www.cccc.org/news_blogs/john/2021/01/11/how-the-church-responded-to-previous-pandemics/.

Peters, Ted. *Playing God: Genetic Determinism and Human Freedom*. 2nd ed. New York: Routledge, 2003.

Peterson, Bailie. "The Concept of God: Divine Attributes." *1000-Word Philosophy*, Sept. 15, 2018. https://1000wordphilosophy.com/2018/09/15/attributes-of-god/.

Phillips, Howard. "'17, '18, '19: Religion and Science in Three Pandemics, 1817, 1918, and 2019." *Journal of Global History* (Nov. 6, 2020) 434–43.

———. *Black October*. Pretoria, South Africa: Government Printer, 1990.

———. "Why Did It Happen? Religious Explanations of the Spanish Flu Epidemic in South Africa." *Historically Speaking* 9.7 (Sept./Oct. 2008) 34–36.

Phillips, Howard, and David Killingray, eds. *The Spanish Influenza Epidemic of 1918–1919: New Perspectives*. London: Routledge, 2003.

Public Domain Review. "15th-Century Illuminations for Dante's Divine Comedy." British Library Catalogue of Illuminated Manuscripts. https://publicdomainreview.org/collection/15th-century-illuminations-for-dante-s-divine-comedy/.

Quinn, Tom. *Flu: A Social History of Influenza*. London: New Holland, 2008.

Rabinowitz, Louis Isaac. "Reward and Punishment." Encyclopedia.com. https://www.encyclopedia.com/religion/encyclopedias-almanacs-transcripts-and-maps/reward-and-punishment.

Reines, Alvin J. "In Medieval Jewish Philosophy: Philosophic Naturalism." Encyclopedia.com. https://www.encyclopedia.com/religion/encyclopedias-almanacs-transcripts-and-maps/reward-and-punishment.

BIBLIOGRAPHY

Remhof, Justin. "'God is dead': Nietzsche and the Death of God." *1000-Word Philosophy*, Feb. 13, 2018. https://1000wordphilosophy.com/2018/02/13/nietzsche-and-the-death-of-god/.

Ritschl, Albrecht. *The Christian Doctrine of Justification and Reconciliation*. Eugene, OR: Wipf & Stock, 2004.

Roberts, Alexander, and James Donaldson, eds. *The Ante-Nicene Fathers*. Vol. 1. New York: Charles Scribner's Sons, 1926.

———. *The Ante-Nicene Fathers*. Vol. 2. New York: Charles Scribner's Sons, 1926.

Robinson, John A. T. *Honest to God*. Philadelphia: Westminster, 1963.

Rolheiser, Ronald. *Domestic Monastery*. Brewster, MA: Paraclete, 2019.

Roy, Arundhati. "The Pandemic Is a Portal." *Financial Times*, Apr. 3, 2020.

Rubenstein, Richard R. *After Auschwitz*. Indianapolis: Bobbs-Merrill, 1969.

———. *The Religious Imagination*. Indianapolis: Bobbs-Merrill, 1968.

Schmitt, Jean-Claude. *The Holy Greyhound*. Cambridge, UK: Cambridge University Press, 1983.

Schnell, Lindsay. "Is the Coronavirus an Act of God? Faith Leaders Debate Tough Questions amid Pandemic." *USA Today*, Apr. 2, 2020. https://www.usatoday.com/story/news/nation/2020/04/02/coronavirus-god-christain-jewish-muslim-leaders-saying-deadly-plague/5101639002/.

Schramm, Percy E. "The Anatomy of a Dictator." In *Hitler: The Man and the Military Leader*, edited by Donald S. Detwiler. Malabar, FL: Robert E. Kreiger, 1978.

Sessa, Kristina. "The Justinianic Plague." *Origins: Current Events in Historical Perspective*, June 2020. https://origins.osu.edu/connecting-history/covid-justinianic-plague-lessons?language_content_entity=en.

Sherman, Paul, and Janet Shellman. "Intelligent Design and the Epiglottis." *Cornell Chronicle*, Dec. 14, 2005. https://news.cornell.edu/stories/2005/12/letter-editor-human-design-and-epiglottis.

Sontag, Frederick. *Divine Perfection*. New York: Harper and Brothers, 1962.

Spinney, Laura. *Pale Rider: The Spanish Flu of 1918 and How It Changed the World*. New York: PublicAffairs, 2017.

Stark, Rodney. *The Rise of Christianity*. Princeton, NJ: Princeton University Press, 1996.

Statista. "Coronavirus (COVID-19) Disease Pandemic—Statistics and Facts." https://www.statista.com/topics/5994/the-coronavirus-disease-covid-19-outbreak/#topic Overview.

Steinweis, Alan E. "The Idea of Eliminating the Leadership Would Not Let Me Rest." The Ina Levine Annual Lecture, United States Holocaust Memorial Museum, December 10, 2018.

Stephen of Bourbon. *De Supersticione: On St. Guinefort*. Internet Medieval Sourcebook, edited by Paul Halsall. https://sourcebooks.fordham.edu/source/guinefort.asp.

Suchocki, Marjorie. *God-Christ-Church: A Practical Guide to Process Theology*. New York: Crossroad, 1982.

Sweeney, Ginia. "Salvation in a Time of Plague." *AMA Journal of Ethics* (May 2020) E441–45. https://journalofethics.ama-assn.org/article/salvation-time-plague/2020-05.

Tennyson, Alfred Lord. *In Memoriam A.H.H.* London: Edward Moxon, 1850.

Thompson, Samantha Elizabeth. "Augustine on Suffering and Order: Punishment in Context." PhD diss., University of Toronto, 2010.

BIBLIOGRAPHY

Thomson, Stuart. "The Birth of a Pandemic: How COVID-19 Went from Wuhan to Toronto." *National Post*, Apr. 8, 2020. https://nationalpost.com/news/politics/the-birth-of-a-pandemic-how-covid-19-went-from-wuhan-to-toronto.

Tillich, Paul. *Systematic Theology.* Vol. 1. Chicago: University of Chicago Press, 1951.

Tippett, Krista. "Elie Wiesel: The Tragedy of the Believer: An Intimate Conversation with Elie Wiesel." *On Being with Krista Tippett*, aired Nov. 20, 2003, on National Public Radio.

Trachtenberg, Joshua. *The Devil and the Jews.* New Haven, CT: Yale University Press, 2012.

Trimbee, Jennifer. "The Spread of the Spanish Flu in 1918." Facty Health, Nov. 16, 2021. facty.com/conditions/medical-history/the-spread-of-the-Spanish-flu-in-1918.

Vaslef, Irene. *The Role of St. Roch as a Plague Saint.* Washington, DC: Catholic University of America Press, 1998.

Vogel, Lawrence, ed. *Mortality and Morality: A Search for the Good After Auschwitz.* Evanston, IL: Northwestern University Press, 1996.

Walsh, Mark. "U.S. Supreme Court Blocks New York State COVID-19 Limits on Religious Services." *Education Week*, Nov. 26, 2020.

Weintrob, Lori R. "Honoring Elie and Marion Wiesel for Their Plays." *Holocaust Theater Catalog*, Apr. 19, 2017. https://htc.miami.edu/elie-wiesels-plays-as-kaddish-the-sacred-duty-to-remember-and-resist/.

Weise, Elizabeth, and Karen Weintraub. "Where Did COVID-19 Come From?" *USA Today*, Jan. 20, 2021.

Wheelis, Mark. "Biological Warfare at the 1346 Siege of Caffa." *Emerging Infectious Diseases* 8.9 (2002) 971–75.

Whitehead, Alfred North. *Adventures of Ideas.* London: Harmondsworth, 1942.

———. *Process and Reality.* Corrected ed. Edited by David Ray Griffin and Donald W. Sherburne. New York: Free Press, 1979.

Wiesel, Elie. *Night.* New York: Hill and Wang, 2006.

———. "The Tragedy of the Believer: An Intimate Conversation with Elie Wiesel." *On Being with Krista Tippett*, aired November 20, 2003. https://onbeing.org/programs/elie-wiesel-the-tragedy-of-the-believer/.

Witchard, Anne. *England's Yellow Peril: Sinophobia and the Great War.* London: Penguin, 2014.

World Health Organization. "Classification of Omicron (B.1.1.529): SARS-CoV-2 Variant of Concern." Nov. 26, 2021. https://www.who.int/news/item/26-11-2021-classification-of-omicron-(b.1.1.529)-sars-cov-2-variant-of-concern.

———. "Novel Coronavirus—China: Disease Outbreak News." Jan. 12, 2020. https://www.who.int/emergencies/disease-outbreak-news/item/2020-DON233.

———. *Report of the WHO-China Joint Mission on Coronavirus Disease 2019.* Feb. 19, 2020.

———. "Weekly Epidemiological Update on COVID-19: Edition 69." Dec. 7, 2021. https://www.who.int/publications/m/item/weekly-epidemiological-update-on-covid-19---7-december-2021.

———. *WHO-Convened Global Study of Origins of SARS-CoV-2: China Part.* Joint WHO-China Study, Mar. 30, 2021.

Worobey, Michael, et al. "The Huanan Seafood Wholesale Market in Wuhan Was the Early Epicenter of the COVID-19 Pandemic." *Science* 377.6609 (July 26, 2022) 951–59.

Worobey, Michael, et al. "A Synchronized Global Sweep of the Internal Genes of Modern Avian Influenza Virus." *Nature* 508 (Feb. 16, 2014) 254–57.

BIBLIOGRAPHY

Wright, N. T. *God and the Pandemic: A Christian Reflection on the Coronavirus and Its Aftermath*. Grand Rapids: Zondervan, 2020.

Wright, Robert. *The Evolution of God*. Boston: Little, Brown, 2009.

Wu, Y. C., et al. "The Outbreak of COVID-19: An Overview." *Journal of the Chinese Medical Association* 83 (3) 217–20.

Yu, Gao, et al. "In Depth: How Early Signs of a SARS-Like Virus Were Spotted, Spread, and Throttled." *Caixin*, Feb. 29, 2020. https://www.caixinglobal.com/2020-02-29/in-depth-how-early-signs-of-a-sars-like-virus-were-spotted-spread-and-throttled-101521745.html.

Yuding, Feng, et al. "In Depth: Tracing the Coronavirus's Origins." *Caixin*, Feb. 5, 2020. https://www.caixinglobal.com/2020-02-05/in-depth-tracing-the-coronaviruss-origins-101511889.html.

Zahnd, Brian. "The Crucified God." *Brian Zahnd* (blog), Mar. 3, 2014. https://brianzahnd.com/2014/03/crucified-god/.

Zentner, McLaurine H. "The Black Death and Its Impact on the Church and Popular Religion." Honors thesis, University of Mississippi, 2015. egrove.olemiss.edu/hon_thesis/682.

Ziegler, Philip. *Black Death*. Glasgow: Williams Collins and Sons, 1969.

Index

Amipotence, 109
Anderson, Bernhard W., 58–60
Armstrong, Dorsey, 1, 24, 90
Aslan, Reza, 90

Barbour, Ian, 87n15, 106
Barth, Karl, 89
Bingen, Hildegard of, 109
Boccaccio, Giovanni, 17–18
Bonhoeffer, Dietrich, 96
Brueggemann, Walter, 60–61
Bubonic plague, theological reactions to, 2, 3, 5, 7, 8, 9, 11–12, 16–20, 95

Calvin, John, 110
Camus, Albert, 55–57
Centers for Disease Control and Prevention (CDC), 43, 44, 45, 47, 49, 51
Chaucer, Geoffrey, 18–19, 57–58
Church, responding in charitable service, 33, 113
Cobb, Jr., John B., 115
Cohn, Norman, 9
Covenant Theology, 58–61, 71, 100
COVID-19, origin of, 38

COVID-19, variants of, 41, 47, 49, 50, 51
COVID-19, theological reactions to, 51–54, 95, 105
Crosby, Alfred, 24, 26, 34

Darwin, Charles, 76–78, 83–84
Defoe, Daniel, 19–21
Deism, xv, 82–84, 100–101
De' Mussi, Gabriele, 3
Dever, William, 107
Devil, 5, 13, 82
Doidge, Norman, 9–10, 16

Epicurus, xiii–xiv, 110
Evolution, xiv, 77–78

Farley, Edward, 117
Fauci, Anthony, 44–45
Flagellants, x, 9–12, 34
Frank, Anne, 68–70

God, as divine parent, 93–94, 104
God, as gardener, 106, 108–9
God, as king, 106–7, 108
God, impassibility of, xi, 115–16, 117

INDEX

God, love of, x, 72, 79, 91, 93–99, 109, 111, 118
God, mystery of, 85, 92, 94, 102–3
God, power of, x–xi, 53–54, 60–61, 68, 69, 72, 74–75, 78–79, 81, 84, 86, 87, 91, 92, 103, 104, 105, 106, 109, 110, 112, 118
God, punishment from, 2, 5, 7, 92
God, wrath of, 3, 7, 10, 27, 52, 94
Great Famine, 4
Grimke, Reverend Francis James, 30–31

Hart, David Bentley, 72–74
Henotheism, 89
Hippo, Augustine of, 74–75, 116
History, Deuteronomistic, 58–61
Hitler, assassination attempt on, 70–71, 96
Holocaust, xiv, xvi, 63–64, 91, 94, 100, 104–5, 113, 117
Honest to God, 87
Horrox, Rosemary, 7
Hume, David, 110

Islam, 21–22, 90

Jesus, 99, 101, 103–4, 111
Jews, scapegoating of, x, 13–16
Jihad, 115
Job, Book of, 62–63, 71–72
Jonas, Hans, 86
Justinian, Emperor, 1–2

Keller, Catherine, 87n15, 106
Kitamori, Kazō, 117
Kohn, George, 14
Kolata, Gina, 24
Kreis, Steven, 10–11
Kushner, Rabbi Harold, 71–72
Kuyper, Abraham, 28

Lactantius, xv
Langland, William, 18
Levi, Primo, 86
Lewis, C.S., 67, 67n29, 79

MacLeish, Archibald, 110
Makarios, Father, 114, 115
Migliore, Daniel, 88n20, 99
Millennialism, 11–12, 29
Miles, Jack, 90–91
Miracles, 82–83
Moltmann, Jürgen, xi, 96, 117
Monotheism, 89–90
Muslims, reactions to pandemics, 21–23, 53n34, 114–15

Newton, John, 78
Nietzsche, Friedrich, 84–85
Night, 64–65, 79, 97
Norwich, Julian of, 109

Oord, Thomas J., xi, 53–54, 97–98, 99, 100, 101, 102, 103, 109

Paley, William, 76–77
Pandemics, conspiracy theories of, 16, 35–36
Pergamum, Galen of, 4
Petrarch (Francesco Petrarca), 16–17
Pilgrimages, 8–9, 33
Plague, saints of, 5–8, 29
Plague, The, 55–57
Polytheism, 8
Prayer, 102, 116–17
Providence, doctrine of, xv, 91–92

Quarantines, 31

Robinson, Bishop John A.T., 87–88
Rubenstein, Rabbi Richard, 63–64, 86, 113

Scapegoating (see also Jews, scapegoating of), 36, 36n72
Science, 12, 28, 30, 33, 34, 35, 37
Science, remedies for the plague, 12–13, 35
Spanish flu, theological reactions to, 26–33, 95
Spillover, zoonotic, 39
Stark, Rodney, 22, 33, 113

INDEX

Tennyson, Alfred Lord, 75–76
Tillich, Paul, 88
Tsunamis, 72–73

Vaughan, Colonel Victor, 26

Whitehead, Alfred North, 106–7, 111
Wiesel, Elie, xi, 64–67, 97

Wisse, Gerard, 28–29
Wright, Bishop N.T., 91, 113
Wright, Robert, 89, 107
Wuhan, 39–40

Yetzers, 114

www.ingramcontent.com/pod-product-compliance
Lightning Source LLC
Chambersburg PA
CBHW072148160426
43197CB00012B/2289